Some Kids I Taught
and
What They Taught Me

Kate Clanchy is a writer, teacher and journalist. Her poetry collection *Slattern* won a Forward Prize. Her short story 'The Not-Dead and the Saved' won both the 2009 BBC National Short Story Award and the VS Pritchett Memorial Prize. Her novel *Meeting the English* was shortlisted for the Costa Prize. Her BBC Radio 3 programme about her work with students was shortlisted for the Ted Hughes prize. In 2018 she was appointed MBE for services to literature, and an anthology of her students' work, *England: Poems from a School*, was published to great acclaim.

KATE CLANCHY

Some Kids I Taught
and
What They Taught Me

PICADOR

First published 2019 by Picador
an imprint of Pan Macmillan
20 New Wharf Road, London N1 9RR
Associated companies throughout the world
www.panmacmillan.com

ISBN 978-1-5098-4029-8

3 5 7 9 8 6 4

A CIP catalogue record for this book is available from the British Library.

Typeset in New Century Schoolbook 9.75/15.75pt by
Palimpsest Book Production Limited, Falkirk, Stirlingshire

Printed and bound by CPI Group (UK) Ltd, Croydon, CR0 4YY

Visit **www.picador.com** to read more about all our books
and to buy them. You will also find features, author interviews and
news of any author events, and you can sign up for e-newsletters
so that you're always first to hear about our new releases.

For my colleagues:
Trish and Emma,
Nikki, Steve and Frank,
Janet,
Cathy, Dee and Annabella,
and all the others.

Contents

Introduction

Thirty years ago, just after I graduated, I started training to be a teacher. As far as I remember, it was because I wanted to change the world, and a state school seemed the best place to start. Certainly, it wasn't a compromise or a stopgap career: I had no thought of being a writer, then.

Soon I was much too busy to write even if I had thought of it. Teacher training is hard, a crash course not so much in the study of education, but in the experience of school: in the taking of the register and the movement of chairs from room to room; in the flooding sounds of corridor and stairs; in the educational seasons, from the tempering heat of exam week to the crazy cosiness of Christmas; and above all in the terrifying confidence trick that is classroom discipline. It's a bodily experience, like learning to be a beekeeper, or an acrobat: a series of stinging humiliations and painful accidents and occasional sublime flights which leave, you either crippled or changed. If you are changed, you are changed for life: your immune system will no longer raise hives when adolescents mock you; you may stand at

1

the door of a noisy classroom with all the calm of a high-wire walker, poised to quell the noise with a twirl of your pole.

Now, I can still confidently tell rowdy adolescents to behave on the bus; still enter a classroom and look at the back row in the indefinable, teacherly way that brings quiet. I still want to change the world and think that school is an excellent place to do it. I have never got tired of classrooms, and have always, except when my children were very young, been employed in some capacity in a state school. Soon after I got my second teaching post, though, I also started to write in my spare time and holidays. A few years later, I began selling some journalism and cut down on my teaching hours; and when I was thirty, I published my first book. Suddenly I found that if I introduced myself in my new guise as a writer I'd be asked what I wrote about, and how, and listened to with a care that seemed exaggerated, even silly. I realized I was accustomed, when I talked about my work, to hardly being listened to at all.

Because everyone tells schoolteachers their jobs: everyone from politicians in parliament and journalists in newspapers to parents at the school concert and pensioners on the bus. The telling ranges from the minutely pedagogical – how we should set, mark, and test; to the philosophical and psychological – how to punish and reward; all the way to the religious – church schools, mindfulness; and politicized issues, such as the reintroduction of grammar schools. The tellings come in the form of laws, political manifestos, editorials, crazed comments in online forums, and – amazingly often – a conversation with someone you have just met. Partly, this happens because people are so interested in schools – most of us were formed there, many of us have children there – but it is also because people feel free to set about a teacher in a way they never would a doctor or a lawyer.

For teachers have a lower social standing than other professionals. This isn't just because we are paid less, as I found out when I entered the even less well remunerated, but far more prestigious, profession of writing. And it isn't just because of the messy, practical nature of teachers' work, either: laymen do not tell a vet how to go about birthing calves, or a gynaecologist where to poke. It may be because so many teachers are women; or perhaps because we work with poor children; and it is certainly because so few of us are posh ourselves (teaching has always been the profession of first resort for graduates from working-class backgrounds). It's because of gender and class prejudice, because, in short, most teachers are *Miss*, as working-class pupils call their female teachers in England.

Miss: I have heard so many professional people express distaste for that name, but never a working teacher. Usually, the grounds are sexism, but real children in real schools don't use 'Miss' with any less (or more) respect than 'Sir'. *Miss* grates only on the ears of those who have never heard it used well: as it grated on me, as a middle-class Scot, thirty years ago. No longer: *Miss* is the name I put on like a coat when I go into school; *Miss* is the shoes I stand in when I call out the kids in the corridor for running or shouting; *Miss* is my cloak of protection when I ask a weeping child what is wrong; *Miss* is the name I give another teacher in my classroom, in the way co-parents refer to each other as 'Mum' or 'Dad'. *Miss* seems to me a beautiful name, because it has been offered to me so often with love.

I would like more people to understand what *Miss* means, and to listen to teachers. Parts of this book, therefore, are a sort of telling-back: long-stewed accounts of how teachers actually do tackle the apostrophe; of how we exclude and include; of the place of religion in schools; of how the many political changes of the last decades have played out in the classroom; of what a demanding, intellectual, highly skilled profession teaching can be. These confident answers, though, are short and few, because mostly what I have found in school is not certainty, but more questions. Complex questions, very often, about identity, nationality, art, and money, but offered very personally: questions embodied in children.

These questions, and the piercing moments when they were presented to me, make up the bulk of this book. It is structured around them: first around the child and the dilemma she brings, then in a wider grouping of related topics, and finally, loosely, around the course of my thirty years in schools, because it is me, not the children, learning the lessons here. I am in each story, clearly delineated, so that you will know what sort of person is doing the listening and filtering, and, I hope, be able to put my views aside and see the kids more clearly. I want to show you us, children and teachers, 'Kids' and 'Miss', both in groups, as if in a long school corridor, and then close in, so you can see the stuff we have brought with us from home, so you can hear some of the things we say.

These are not biographies: they are partial views of young people absorbed in their circumstances, on the move, on the cusp, on the turn. But, even in a snapshot, children have the right to privacy just as adults do; and, more strongly than adults, the right to leave their old selves behind them. So, even where the stories are the most admiring, and when individuals positively wanted to be identified, I have detached these accounts from their original names, times, and places. Some stories need more privacy, and I have provided that with occasional very extensive blurring of identity. I have quoted one or two poems, and named two poets, from the anthology of my students' poems, *England: Poems from a School*, and used, with express permission, one real name from my past; other than that, no named individual here should be identified as any particular living person. I hope, however, that offence would not be given even if a general identification were made, because I have included nobody, teacher or pupil, about whom I could not write with love.

There is so much to love in school. I am writing this in September, school's New Year. I am snug in my study, writing: I would rather be in school. Teaching has taken me a long journey out of my class, and my nation; it takes me, every time I go in, out of myself. Today, the corridors are full of the young, of new pupils, and of old pupils renewed. Things have happened to them over the summer: they are different, experimental people, full of themselves, eager to tell me about it. The register is fresh with names; the exercise books are crunched open at the spine, the pages blank and smooth as Larkin's spring leaves. *Begin afresh*, they seem to say. *afresh, afresh*. I fall for it, every year. You come too.

About Love, Sex, and the Limits of Embarrassment

Callum, Paul, Liam, Akash, Emmanuel, and Javel

Callum's Dog

To begin at the very beginning, with sperm and egg, with condoms and cucumbers, with ghastly line drawings of urethras and sperm ducts, and me, just starting out as a teacher. To go all the way back to the very early nineties, and to a small town on the east coast of Scotland. The Tories had been in power since way before I could vote, and Section 28, which notoriously forbade the 'promoting' of homosexuality in schools, was still law. These were the just-post-Thatcher years, and the mining industry in Scotland was a warm corpse, a popped boil, its raw red bings and destroyed communities disfiguring the central belt. They were the *Trainspotting* years, when drugs were rampant in the estates of Edinburgh, hundreds had died of infected needles, and thousands more were infected with HIV.

And so, one fine day, the High Heejuns, as the powers that be are called in Scotland, looked at this toxic list of miseries, and decided that Something Must be Done, and, as usual, that the Something would probably be easiest and cheapest done in schools. Education, then and now, is far more centralized in Scotland than in England, so it was not long before books, schemes of work, and acetate illustrations for that then-cutting-edge piece of classroom equipment, the overhead projector, were on their way to Blastmuir High School, where I had a temporary job, and to the muggins in charge of the target group of thirteen-year-olds: me.

Lord, how young I was – twenty-four, and in my fluffy-haired photos I look even younger. My Second Years, though, still looked like children to me, even though they were entering their teens: all of them so short, so hunched in their wee anoraks. My eye was tuned in to the multi-racial London pupils I'd taught the year before, who had, by the same age, Somali height or Cypriot bosoms or styled, stiff Japanese hair, or at the very least a different, flam-boyant way with the school jumper. These winter-coloured, mouse-haired children, so pale and so freckly, with their muttering, sibilant names – Fraser, Struan, Susan, Fiona, Catriona; I was having difficulty, as Prince Philip said he had with Chinese people, in telling them apart.

Or in teaching them, really. It wasn't that I couldn't keep them quiet – on the contrary, if I was stern and cold, they were easy to bid – it was that I couldn't get them to talk. In London, I had become used to vocal children, from talking cultures: Turkish girls who, halfway through a test or a telling-off, stroked your jacket and asked you where you got it; multi-lingual, super-sophisticated Ugandan Asians who would raise their hands to answer any question with a full paragraph; Jewish 'becks' with swathes of curly hair who turned every classroom into a friendly street corner where the neighbourhood was debating the great issues of the day. My lessons, there, turned always on acting out and making up – if there wasn't a chance to divide into small groups and perform a scene, preferably with a dance and original song included, my London pupils saw it as an hour wasted.

In Blastmuir, these lessons failed spectacularly. 'How?' the Blastmuir kids begged, if I asked them to interpret four lines of *Macbeth*. 'Act it out how?' And, if I forced the issue, they would come to the front, stand in a row and read the lines in a very fast monotone, to their socks. They didn't dance, here. They knew no songs. My London students had spent their lunchtimes plaiting each other's hair, their hands always on each other, cuddling and stroking. Blastmuir kids didn't touch. Instead, small boys paced the corridors alone with outsize bags; outside class, boys and girls stood in ranks, backs to opposite walls, as if at an eighteenth-century dance. The older boys played football, aggressively, out on the muddy field with those vast sports bags as goalposts, or walked to the chip shop down the long straight high street in groups of four. And if the older girls applied each other's bright blue eyeshadow, or adjusted the pink stripes of blusher on one another's freckly cheeks, or added more hairspray to their pale and rigid hair, they must have done so secretly, in the steel toilets, behind the bashed Formica walls, for I never saw it happen.

Even in the staffroom, teachers sat in divided rows, in high-backed chairs permanently dented by particular bottoms. Staff busied themselves rather than talk. One teacher explained to me that the stitching in her hand was a patchwork Christmas tree: they were such popular gifts that she had to start each Easter to have enough to give away at Christmas. 'Och,' sighed a melancholy lady who proved to be the Head of French, 'och, I can't abide an orange. It's such a messy froot.' And I longed for an orange, suddenly, in that green and khaki Nescafé-smelling room where we were stitching for Christmas, if only to prove this was 1992, and not the war.

Blastmuir kids, I decided, were better than my London students at just two things: spelling 'wh' sounds, for they had a strong, hooting 'h' in their speech that made 'where' and 'which' entirely different from 'were' and 'witch'; and keeping a straight face while hissing deadly insults at each other from half-closed mouths. This I learned to cultivate: maybe Blastmuir kids wouldn't make things up, but they loved a formal debate. I found that with a little push you could create a literary argument: for example, between Macduff and Macbeth. Across the classroom, they hissed and hooted Scandinavian syllables at each other, flyting in the style of Thor and Odin: 'Macbeth, you cannae be king. You're no the right sort. Youse is a scaffie wee schemie, so youse are.'

'Scaffie' meant grubby, uncared for; and 'schemie' one who lived in a council housing scheme, as opposed to your 'ain hoose'. This was an important distinction to my Blastmuir students, one always visible to them however invisible it might be to me, and often raised in class. 'Schemie' was a grave insult, but it had nothing on the comeback: 'Macduff, youse and Banquo is gayboys and youse know it.' For 'gay' was Blastmuir's biggest word: its enforcer word; the category into which no one would put themselves. It didn't mean homosexual, exactly, or not just that: it meant foreign, citified; it meant dancing, touching; it meant making things up; it meant *verboten*, un-Scottish, *haram*.

'Gay' also meant, I suppose, in origin: 'unwilling to go down the pit'; 'too soft to go down the pit'; 'his mother doesn't want him to go down the pit'; 'believes he can avoid going down the pit just by being clever'; and, ultimately, 'sensitive in a way that terrifies his parents because they remember all too well how much it hurts'. But I didn't understand that, then. Even though I had grown up only a few miles away, in Edinburgh, I knew nothing about mining towns: nothing of how proud and macho a culture has to be, how strongly enforced, how rigorously starved of other possibilities, if generations of men are to be pushed down into the hot dark to work themselves to death. Nothing, either, of the demands that mining families must place on their children to honour their father's extreme sacrifice: nothing, really, about Blastmuir. I only knew the town after the mine and its work, money, dignity, and purpose had been withdrawn. I knew the brittle husk of culture it left behind, and how to despise it.

But at least my ignorance meant I didn't worry too much about the AIDS book and the acetates from the council. Anti-gay prejudice, I airily assumed, was something everyone would grow out of, really, quite soon; and anyway, the book and the lessons would probably not even connect to the kids' anti-'gay' prejudices, because the acetates really were all about bodies, not the wider, cultural meaning of 'gay'. I had taught bodies and Sex Ed before without difficulty, even the cucumber and condom bit, and to less docile children. Explaining the workings of HIV, I reckoned, would probably be an easy lesson, with everyone at once fairly interested and too embarrassed to talk.

Besides, the AIDS book was well chosen, and the kids were enthusiastic as we read it cosily round the class: a sunny, funny Australian novel about a little boy whose mum is ill, and who falls into conversation with a nice man in the hospital. Until we got to the well-placed twist; that is, when of course we realized that the nice man has AIDS, that's why he's in the hospital, and that all his kindly wisdom about mortality comes from a personal source. Page 78. I had it ready marked. I had one of the council-prepared acetates on the overhead projector, which I had booked in advance and even plugged in. The acetate had 'AIDS' in big letters on the top. Page 77. Here we go. I swivelled to switch on the machine. It roared cheerfully.

But when I turned back around, I realized that the front row had closed their books, and put them away from them on the desks. 'Hey,' I said. 'We're not finished yet. Keep your bookmarks in.' But the children behind them had closed their books too. They weren't rioting, or even giggling: just refusing to read the book.

Then a wee girl said, 'Mrs Clanchy,' (they don't say 'Miss' in Scotland; sometimes the children even called me 'Mrs McClanchy' as if 'Mc' were part of a teacher's title too), 'Mrs Clanchy, we cannae read this. We dinnae want to catch AIDS.' So I turned off the overhead projector, and tried to talk to them about it.

It took me a while to credit it wasn't a nasty joke: they genuinely thought the book might infect them. It took me longer to take in that I had been much too right about the use of the term 'gay'. Not only did the kids use the word independently of any connection with homosexuality, most of them believed that homosexuality did not exist as a bodily phenomenon at all. They thought it was just a badness, an idea of infective evil. And it took me all the way till the end of the lesson to realize that in that room of thirteen-year-olds, only one or two were confident even of the mechanics of sex; and most of my way home on the bus to believe it. Dear God, I thought, as we swung into Edinburgh. Oh dear.

Because then I also remembered that I had promised that I would explain everything, next lesson. Everything about sex, that is, all of it, to all of Blastmuir. I had said that anyone in the class who had a question about sex should write it down anonymously and put it in a box on my desk beforehand, and I, Kate, currently disguised as Mrs McClanchy, would tell them the answer. And then, perhaps, I would be arrested, and deported back to London. Or staked out on a bing to be pecked to death by crows. Or die of shame, whichever was quicker.

Why did I say that? Where did I get that idea? I can't remember. I can only suppose that this was a tactic suggested to me in training sometime; or maybe even on the dreaded council advice sheet. I remember I did not sleep the following night. I remember wearing a smart jacket into the lesson, as if that would defend me. I remember the fear of going into that rigid classroom. I remember it every time people ask me now, when I am about to address a large hall, if I am not afraid; or, when I write about my life, if I am not embarrassed. I remember it, because in relation to that hour, I have never been afraid or embarrassed since.

But look, the kids were eager, quiet, already in their seats, a pile of slips in the box on the desk. They fell silent as I picked the first question out. It was, 'What do gay people actually do for sex?' and I took a breath, and, cautiously, as if I were setting foot for the first time on ice of unknown thickness, said sex was the same whatever you did and whoever you did it with. It was about touching and feeling and also feelings, and people did all sorts of things.

Then I looked round the room and saw that the kids were carefully not looking at each other, but at me. No one had sniggered. And so, as if putting another skate on the ice and feeling the bowl of the lake wobble beneath my feet, I set off, finding purchase for my blade. I said the words 'clitoris', 'penis' and 'erection' in a single brief paragraph. *Schoosh, schoosh.* I'm a good skater; I learned when I was young. I can go backwards as easily as forwards and brake on a sixpence.

I said 'orgasm'. Someone laughed, but it was a nice laugh. Aye, said someone else, aye, I see.

I picked the next question from the pile: what happens if you are having sex and you want to have a pee? I drew on the board. I made sure they knew the difference between vagina and urethra. I explained what a foreskin was, and that it was possible to have sex while menstruating and that you could use a tampon even if you were a virgin and that everyone masturbates and has wet dreams. Mostly, though, the questions were not about juices, but about love: could anybody love; could gay people love; could you change, later on? I only had to say the words aloud, and say yes.

The sun came in through the seventies windows and warmed us all. The stiff children of Blastmuir eased back from their desks or leant cheerfully across them. Eyes met mine which had never done so before, small Scottish mouths hung open, eager for more information to be spooned in. I felt as if I were in a different classroom: as if we had travelled through the looking glass to a new country, the one beyond embarrassment.

In fact, all children will behave perfectly, I believe, if they want to know something very much, about sex or anything else, and an adult sincerely sets out to tell them. And most humans, whatever prejudices they avow, will set them aside when difference is made real in a person. (If, that is, they are not afraid.) But I didn't know that then: that was when I learned it.

At the end of the lesson, Callum came up to me. Callum, in a class of undersized, underdeveloped children, by far the least tall, the least developed. Callum with the heavy eyelids, the lopsided face, the slack jaw.

'Mrs McClanchy?' said Callum.

'Yes?'

'Whit wis the name for men and men?'

'That was homosexuality, Callum.'

'Aye. And whit wis the name for women and men?'

'That's heterosexuality, Callum.'

'Aye. Well, when I grow up, I'm no' going to have either o' them. Ah think Ah'll just have a big dog.'

No one said 'fluid' then – gender-fluid, fluid identity – but fluid is a good word for that afternoon. The room seemed liquid, lacking in barriers. And fluid was what those children were, behind their stern names and rigid codes. Changeable, molten, and warm as any child; waiting for a mould, hoping there would be space for the swelling, shrinking and unknowable quantity of themselves. For Callum, that space needed to include the possibility of living on his own, and that was as important to him as the possibility, for surely one child in that class, and very probably more, of falling in love with someone of your own sex. So, I didn't say that would be bestiality, Callum, though the thought flickered across my mind. I said yes, yes, Callum, you could do that. A dog would be very nice. That, Callum, would be grand.

Paul's Boots

After Blastmuir, I went to work in its (distorting) mirror-image, its English opposite, the Essex conurbation to the east of London; a place which had grown as fast as Blastmuir had shrunk, whose industries – finance, construc-tion, services – were as thriving and Thatcherite as Blastmuir's mines were redundant and Old Labour. *Gavin & Stacey*, the ascendency of Nigel Farage, and above all the television series *TOWIE*, have now made this bit of Essex, with its nightclubs and vajazzles, nationally famous. Then, it was not; though its ferociously strong consumerist culture was every bit as distinctive.

My college was brand new: the first sixth-form college in an area where kids had traditionally left school at sixteen. But most of this area was new – or at least post-war. The nearest town looked like a Middle American city: mall-centred, concrete, with long streets lined with semis. The kids looked Middle American too: plump and handsome and tow-headed; better set up than the Blastmuir kids, and much more showily dressed. Boys here wore pink – pastel polo shirts, buttoned up to the neck, very clean – and had pierced ears and sometimes noses, and one lad, a Prince Albert ring (at least, he passed round the receipt). Girls had sprayed hair and full make-up and push-up bras, and both sexes wore multiple gold chains round their necks, often with letters spelling out their names; and several rings on both hands, chunky gold ones, diamond chip ones, and ones with initial letters deep set, as if ready for the delivery of an 'Essex kiss'.

Also, miniature solitaires, for engagements were commonplace. So was sex. Those were the years of the Essex girl joke: How does an Essex girl put out the light after sex? She closes the car door. How can you tell if an Essex girl has had an orgasm? She drops her chips. The kids told these jokes cheerfully, with pride, and if they weren't all having sex in cars most nights, they certainly all went regularly to the local nightclubs and talked freely about it; it was an approved-of, almost compulsory activity, something you did with your friends and cousins and even your mum. Many of these sixteen- and seventeen-year-olds had long-standing boyfriends and girlfriends, and brought them home to stay with their parents. The generation gap, in general, was narrow and blurred: parents turned up to parents' evenings and enrolment events wearing the same brash jewellery and sportswear as their children, and, in the face of reports and university forms, displayed much the same mixture of ostentatious indifference and chronic anxiety.

In fact, this was one of our big problems: school had never done much – or even tried to do much – for the Essex parents; now, it was hard to persuade their children that it could do something for them. For these were kids who did not want to rebel against their parents: it was too comfy at home. One of our favourite texts was Willy Russell's *Stags and Hens*, a funny, soppy play about working-class Liverpudlians in a nightclub. The dialect was unfamiliar, but the set-up – rigidly divided genders from a loving but limited working-class culture, stuck forever in a nightclub – made perfect sense to our students. The only problem came with the denouement, when the heroine makes the decision to leave her home and possible marriage for a more adventurous life. Even at the supposedly rebellious age of seventeen, even when the heroine was being offered a rock star, our students generally thought she should stay at home and marry, just as, when we were studying the War Poets, they still thought conscription was a good idea.

So that made literary discussion hard. Also, I kept coming up against strange blanks, walls of absolute ignorance such as who Adam and Eve might be, and what was the Garden of Eden. My A Level class thought Queen Victoria was 'the one with the red hair and the pearls'. When I read Herbert's 'The Flower' I was driven to uproot a daffodil, just to show them what a root was, and a stem. More than that, though, and more than any other kids I've taught before or since, they didn't want to enquire about books, or relate them to themselves. Teaching *Othello* to Asian and Turkish girls in North London had been easy because they knew what racism was and what an honour code meant: the play opened them to talking about their home cultures and often to criticizing them. In Essex, whether the text was Orwell or Thomas Hardy, the students refused to relate them to their families; yet all of them must have come to this town from somewhere else within a couple of generations, whether from fields like Hardy or cities like Orwell.

At first, when I started out with classes here, I tried my favourite introductory game: asking the students where their name came from. In North London, this gave you an instant cultural history of the child: the Hindu horoscope that had been calculated for them, or, from a Nigerian girl: 'My name is Osla. I am the last of seven children, and my name means "Enough".' In Blastmuir, it often yielded a close, proud family history: there, children were still named for relatives, and boys after their mother's maiden name. In Essex, though, the kids fiercely denied that their names had any history or meaning at all. I was baffled when a boy with jet-black hair and eyes and a fine Ashkenazi nose named David Marks refused any Jewish heritage, or when a freckled Irish-eyed kid called O'Riordan declared he'd never heard of Dublin. The few mixed-race kids were even more aggressively shut down, rejecting any kind of ancestor, Caribbean or otherwise. 'I'm normal, Miss,' they'd say. 'Normal.'

But what did they think normal was? I asked my tutor group what percentage of the population of the UK they thought was non-white. About 75 per cent, they replied, firmly, without hesitation. Why did they think that? It's what you see, they said. Did they? How could they, when they were so white?

It was only slowly, over years spent travelling back from college to my home in Spitalfields, that I saw what they meant. As you left their part of Essex and went west into London through Dagenham and Tower Hamlets, people became more and more mixed. Beyond Walthamstow, people really were 75 per cent of colour, and came from all over the world. When my Essex students went anywhere, they went the same way as me: west, the direction of their parents' commute; and so the land to the west, the wildly mixed East End of London, was what they thought constituted the rest of England. The East End was also the place their parents had left, or, often, perceived themselves to have been displaced from by new immigrants, or to have worked their way out of using their grit and endurance: in all these stories, white Essex figured as the Promised Land.

So urban Essex really was like America: a new, colonial country, and like all new cultures, it was self-conscious and brittle. David Marks and Sean O'Riordan probably were just two generations out of Spitalfields or Stepney, seven from a potato famine or a pogrom, but their families didn't want to remember that, not any more, because then they wouldn't belong in Essex, wouldn't fit in its narrow 'normal'. There could be nothing gender-fluid about such a 'normal' either, for all the bling, pizzazz and pink inherited from the Cockney markets; any deviance was threatening. There was nothing slipshod here, nothing worn-in or grubby; the whole place was as stiff as new shoes. And so, for all the sexual precocity, 'gay' was as much of an enforcing word here as ever it was in Blastmuir, and if it did not include male ornamentation, it still definitely covered theatre and singing. It had a special geographical sense too, which coincided with the prevailing racial prejudice: inner London and its activities, except 'The City', where many aspired to work, was 'gay'.

Paul, then, was an oddity, and a refreshment. He was taking a Drama qualification with GCSEs in German and Media Studies on the side. He was tall and slender with floppy, dark-red hair and sleepy eyes. He wore cashmere jumpers, turned-up trousers, and a single earring, and slinked about, curling up on desks and tables like a cat. If you said, 'Good morning,' he would roll his eyes and say, 'Good? if you say so,' and pout, for he was dedicated entirely to camp (school of John Inman, not Susan Sontag).

At first, I assumed this knowing manner meant he was also ironical and clever, and that the re-sit GCSEs were some sort of mistake; but, as I got to know him, this proved not to be the case. Paul was expert at catching my tone, and giving me an encouraging wink, but his punctuation was poor and his essays no better than anyone else's. He hadn't read anything and didn't intend to. He didn't know the cultural references that went with his sophisticated manner, neither Stonewall nor Spartacus. He was resolutely non-political: Section 28, the gathering point for almost all gay activism then, seemed to mean nothing to him at all.

Paul knew one thing, though, and that was how to keep himself safe. Somehow, in the Essex world, there was a place for camp just as there was a place for pink: a small one. Paul was considered hilarious, and his camp remarks were roared at even when they had scarcely any content. Bizarrely enough, he was not considered 'gay', and was welcomed in all social groups – though he did seem to slip in and out of them, making his jokes, then disappearing before anyone could tire of him. He went, it seemed, to the nightclubs with the rest of them, for his dancing was legendary, and somehow, so well had he established the myth of himself, nobody thought it strange that he always danced alone.

He knew musicals, too, both from watching them on videos and going to the West End. He induced the Drama teacher to put on *Cabaret*, with which he was particularly obsessed, and dominated the stage as the Master of Ceremonies, pouncing and posing: *Life is a cabaret, old chum. Come to the cabaret.* The three-day run of the play was evidently an ecstatic experience for him; he was pale and exalted in all lessons and handed in no work for a month.

'Is that what you really want to do, Paul?' I asked. 'Theatre?'

'Oh no,' he said. 'No. I just like that musical. I wanted

to do that. Not the real thing.' And his Drama teacher, surprisingly – since *Cabaret* was the best show the college had ever put on – agreed. Paul had, she said, no range at all, no capacity to read or explore a play, and not much of a voice; he could just dance, quite well, and be camp, amazingly well. Paul was no David Bowie, or Boy George, though his non-conformity probably came from the same source.

After the play, Paul turned his attention to Media Studies. This was mostly coursework (a viable system in those far-off, pre-internet days) and it ended with a major project. Before Photoshop, pre-YouTube, such projects were daft, amateur, and creative: hand-painted advertising campaigns for imaginary perfumes; laboriously typed newspapers. The college video camera, though, was most in demand. Stop motion animations advertising ice creams were popular, as were 'promo' videos in the style of MTV. Videos were supposed to last a maximum of ten minutes. Paul, though, declared he wanted to make a horror film.

He recruited a cameraman and sidekick, the pale and silent Tony. He created a script. The film, he declared, would 'explore the genre of horror by performing it', and it would star an aluminium trolley from the science department, the college lift, and a good deal of tomato ketchup. In a series of low, long shots influenced by *The Shining*, the trolley would sweep the college corridors, looking for victims. In the style of *The Birds*, it would hypnotize a blonde girl into the lift using tweeting noises (Tony, on a water-filled plastic bird whistle). The doors would close, and more sinister bubbling noises would be heard, and then, in a reference to *Carrie*, the lift would be opened and found to be covered with blood. Finally, the trolley, still aiming low, would be chased down the corridors in *Hammer House of Horror* style by the ever-useful Tony – armed with a water pistol – and apprehended.

Making something as ambitious as this took weeks and required much pre-booking of the camera. I got fond of the boys, though, through the process. Tony had ideas and patience of his own, and, unlike Paul, always listened to what I suggested. He painstakingly made a set of stop motion credits for the film, in which Plasticine blood leaked through bars and formed itself into letters: *Night of the Killer Trolley*. The letters got up on their feet and ran away. He pushed Paul into actually writing the project's compulsory accompanying commentary, and got it to pass-able length and depth – though Paul did insist on writing it in pink ink and sprinkling it with references to 'friends of Dorothy'. As for Paul himself, I could not but admire his tenacity; he was prepared to spend three hours getting a single trolley shot right. And his good nature was steel-plated, ocean-going: Five in the evening? Six? 'No problem, Kate, you know you want to be here really. I'm your very favourite student.' By then, he probably was.

The final film was smooth, and clever, and deeply silly, and altogether more than the sum of its parts. The exam board, who must have been short on laughs that year, commented that they had never seen anything quite like it, and gave it an A. That was the first A of any kind that Paul had ever got in school, and when he found out in September, he and Tony went out and bought me a large box of Roses chocolates, and we all sat a while in my late summer classroom, sucking on strawberry creams.

The boys weren't coming back to school; they had both, they said, got jobs in Marks & Spencer. I made no attempt, despite the A, to persuade either of them to reconsider and do A Levels. Tony had never had academic pretensions; and it was hard to imagine a better venue for Paul and his curious portfolio of talents than a large shop, where he could sail the escalators, approve shirts, and tighten trousers, where he could focus forever, indefatigably, on the frivolous. Besides, Paul seemed so happy. He regaled me with the tale of his holiday: how he and Tony had got jobs by the seaside and bought an ancient car and driven it to Le Touquet, where it broke, terminally, so they'd had to hitch home. How they stayed up later and later each night until they became nocturnal animals, and only communicated with their parents by Post-it note, left on the fridge.

'Haven't seen them for weeks, have we, Tone?' said Paul.

It was the image of the yellow Post-it, trembling on the fridge, which let me know that the boys were lovers, probably had been for months, hiding in plain sight in this hostile environment. I was filled with admiration; without politics, without adult help, and seemingly without damage, these boys had defeated the rigid prohibitions that surrounded them. Like the children of Blastmuir, they were fluid, really. Like Tony's Plasticine letters, they had magically poured themselves through the bars and re-formed in the shape of their happiness; hopped into an ancient, uninsured car and driven off forever. Rage against Essex would almost certainly come later; rage was deserved. For now, they had M&S, and the beach at Le Touquet.

'Look,' said the normally silent Tony, stretching out a leg with a camp, brightly laced Doc Marten at the end of it. 'My boots. They're exactly the same as Paul's.'

'Yes?' I said. Their turned-up jeans were identical too.

'But,' said Tony, 'we wasn't together when we bought them! We was in two different shops at the same time and we bought the same boots!'

'Telepathy,' said Paul. 'You see, Kate?' And I agreed that telepathy was what it must be.

Liam's Club

'Gay'. Four years into working at my college – I stayed there seven years, I loved my boss and my colleagues – 'gay' had become my shorthand for all the interdictions of Essex, and I hated it with a far-from-academic passion. 'Gay' was the reason only girls could study English Literature, and boys who liked words had to take English Language and Media Studies. 'Gay' was the threat that stopped boys studying foreign languages. (The Head of French really was gay, perhaps a double-edged sword.) 'Gay' stopped us reading Carol Ann Duffy; 'gay' made parents complain on parents' evening that I was disturbing their child's mind. 'Gay' stopped boys coming to Poetry Group; 'gay' stopped poetry full stop. 'Gay' was the dam in the stream, the opposite of fluid, the opposite of thought, and it made teaching English A Level in particular very hard because when it comes right down to it, all great literature is subversive.

And damn it, I'd always wanted to teach A Level English Literature. Actually, I'd always wanted to *study* an A Level; I did Scottish Higher, in a class of twenty-five sitting in iron forms in alphabetical order. A Level, I believed, was the opposite: a lounging, japing, delightful sort of course. Not in Essex. A Levels were designed in the 1950s for grammar schools, for at most 10 per cent of the school population, a pre-university course. Despite alterations, this was not suitable for our college; for the 50 per cent or so of the school population who'd got a C or B grade at GCSE, who sat waiting for enlightenment in classes of twenty or more. There was no lounging involved, just heaps of marking and a lot of C grades.

Perhaps, I thought, sourly, perhaps japing and lounging still occurred in the famous grammar school half a mile down the road, the school that sucked up all the bright middle-class kids in the area, leaving us with the resentful leftovers. Perhaps in the grammar school, in the proper conditions, among ten bright pupils sitting round the library table of a sunny afternoon, *Othello* was still fun. In our place, with the 90 per cent of the population who cannot see the point of literary criticism, it was uphill all the way.

'Kids – why does Iago hate Othello? Doesn't he love him, a little? "He hath a daily beauty in his life that makes me ugly" . . . Don't we all sometimes hate people as well as love them, desire as well as like our friends . . .' What I meant was, please relax your judgements, just for a moment. Please. Let yourselves think. But it was impossible. The kids doing re-sit GCSE, I found, were more open-minded, probably because they were less successful at Essex life, and therefore had less to protect. I started to teach more and more GCSE; the year of Tony and Paul, I opted for it as my entire timetable.

And then I met Jane and Liam. They appeared side by side at the back of my only English Literature class: a thin boy with lively eyes and a long mouth; a smooth, blonde girl with lowered lashes. They had both come from one of our roughest feeder schools, and though Liam sometimes raised his eyes and grinned at one of my jokes, they seemed to have acquired there the art of keeping their heads down. They only answered questions when I directly named them; otherwise they discussed each point of the lesson between themselves, in a practised, discreet whisper.

When I took their first essays in, I learned why they were undercover. Jane was clever to a point that must have made daily difficulties for her: clever in the marshalled, exact, mercilessly perceptive way particularly threatening in a girl. Liam was even more of an outlier. He had adult, italic handwriting, and an adult, cool tone; a voice sprang from his pages, a funny, knowing one. And while Jane's essay was a perfect digest of what she had been taught, plus a few thoughtful observations of her own – the very pattern of an A grade – Liam's was almost perversely his own: an odd, elegant, original argument about *Jane Eyre*, ornamented with such strange, yet deftly plucked and trimmed quotations, that I wondered if he had been secretly attending an entirely different set of lessons.

Nevertheless, two bright students actually ready for

A Level: a miracle. I set out to cultivate them as bright A Level students are traditionally cultivated: the lending of books, the suggesting of outings, the casual chatting at the end of class. This immediately misfired. Jane found my friendliness suspicious, perhaps patronizing. She was, I slowly discovered, very much a working-class girl, very close to her single mother and her extended family. Jane had applied to the grammar school at eleven, but because the school operated a nakedly snobbish system of interviewing the parents, rather than the child, she had been denied a place. Since then, Jane and her mother had less faith in teachers, and her cleverness had become a secret project for the two of them. Together, carefully, they were working out how Jane might go to university, which no member of their family had ever done, and how she might even study English, a subject which seemed of no practical use. They were doing fine, as they would just about allow me to affirm. They did not want any other help.

As for Liam, he was simply unclubbable. He refused to do even the few things I inveigled Jane into – not for him the extra project, the Cambridge trip, the theatre visit. He dropped out of Maths. He never, after that first effort, handed in work on time or on topic. In the second year of A Levels, Jane visited several universities, applied, was accepted; while Liam refused even to fill in a UCAS form. Nevertheless, I persisted, setting an extra, ironical Liam question at the bottom of every worksheet, making special little Liam cracks in class, leaving out piles of books to be picked up: the Morse code, underwater signals of the oddball to the oddball, one writerly mind to the other. It worked:

he did get cleverer and cleverer; he did write more and more fluent and lengthy and eccentric essays, full of perceptions that made me laugh out loud; he really was the best and funniest literary critic I'd ever taught, the best I was ever going to teach. He made my lessons worth planning, my job worth doing. And slowly, in his last year, he did start hanging around at the end of lessons, A4 file clutched to his chest, and he did start chatting from one side of his long mouth, and I did find out where he came from.

Liam wasn't a grammar school reject; his parents weren't organized or aspirational enough to have even applied. They had split up lengthily and painfully in his early teens, leaving him, an only child, very much to his own devices. All his bookishness – and he read passionately – was his own invention, an irregular breadcrumb trail traced through libraries and schoolteachers. He had taken to the Essex life of new clothes and nightclubs early, then abandoned it. Now, he spent his time with other lost children, particularly a girl called Meredith with whom I assumed he was in love, in an alternative Essex of empty houses and rotting swimming pools, small-time criminals and night-time parks; like misfits from an American movie; like Damon Albarn out of Blur, with whom he was naturally obsessed; like Jarvis Cocker and *A Different Class*, album of the year, which, as Liam said, was 'just like you, Kate, ain't it, slumming it down here'. Thanks for that, Liam.

Even a very alternative Essex, though, didn't seem like the place to spend what I persisted in calling a gap year, and Liam seemed sure was the rest of his life. What was wrong with the boy? He didn't, unlike Jane, have a cherished place in a cherished family to lose. His critique of Essex and its values was far more developed than mine. He yearned, it seemed, for travel. Why didn't he take the simple escape route so cheaply available to him, and apply to university – if not Cambridge, then at least London, just down the road? Why couldn't he knuckle down to study? What was holding him back?

'Ain't you guessed?' said Liam. It was after the school end-of-term do, after all the exams. Teachers and eighteen-year-old students grandly ordering pints in a terrible Essex pub. 'Seriously, don't you know?'

He was truly disappointed. 'You,' he said furiously, 'you lent me *Tales of the City*. Do you know how much I loved those books?'

'That was for the Dickens project,' I said feebly. Though it had really been for my anti-Essex project. I'd thought of Armistead Maupin as the most metropolitan and hopeful text a young person was likely to actually read.

'They are so gay,' said Liam accusingly.

And, of course, they are. And so, of course, was Liam. I had made another mistake with 'gay', just as I had in Blastmuir. This time, I had been determined that a literary, ironical, and artistic boy, a desperate romantic with delicate perceptions and tender feelings, could be just as heterosexual as the next. Besides, Liam wasn't camp in the least.

'Sorry, Liam,' I said, 'really sorry. You're with girls all the time.'

'Girls,' said Liam, 'are nicer. But I fancy boys.' And he started to talk fluently, fluidly, his reserve finally gone, the mature, funny voice of the essays at last inhabiting the skinny boy. He was determined to come out, but it was terrifying. This was the battle that had taken up all his energy while Jane worked out if she could go to university. This was why he had distanced himself from Jane, his academic twin since primary school. This was the concern that had taken his focus: who to tell, what they might say, and what might happen. So far, he hadn't told his friends, nor his parents, nor Jane – just his underworld friends, the strange Meredith, and now, me.

It was late, and we stared at each other across the emptying pub. The students were off somewhere they could drink more: the Essex nightclubs, most likely. 'What should we do?' I asked. 'To celebrate your coming out?'

Liam took a breath. He said, 'Do you know any gay clubs?'

I didn't, really. My friend Colette had taken me to a couple of lesbian bars in Islington, but I didn't think that was what he had in mind.

'Don't you,' he said, 'even know G-A-Y?' And I did. Everyone knew that one.

'OK,' said Liam, 'we'll go there for a drink.'

'No,' I said, 'I can't do that.'

'Why not,' said Liam. 'Really, why? I'm eighteen.'

'I'm your teacher,' I said weakly. 'It's not right.'

'You're not my teacher any more,' said Liam firmly.

I was, though. That was our relationship. I couldn't take him to a gay nightclub. Any nightclub.

'Kate,' said Liam. 'You actually have to. Because no one in Essex knows where it is.'

And that was also true, then. It was the early nineties,

and we navigated London using A–Z Maps and the listings at the back of *Time Out* magazine. It was intimidating to a university-educated twenty-something on a good day. Then there weren't smartphones and satellite maps. There weren't YouTube videos and websites. So Liam had no map. Essex had set its face against Soho and everything it meant, and I was the only person in Liam's world who could guide him there.

'Now?' I said, quailing.

'Now,' said Liam. 'Don't panic. I'm only going to go in, and have a little dance, and come out again.'

So we got on the tube, and sat opposite each other all the wobbling way into London, grinning from time to time. I guided Liam through the dark streets of London to G-A-Y and paid his entrance fee. He was shaking, and I pointed this out.

'Are you surprised?' he said. 'I ain't done this before.'

Inside it was roaring, smoky and dark, with men in tight T-shirts dancing close together. I made my way to a bar and got two plastic cups of beer. Liam disappeared into the crowd, and I felt a new kind of pain, a physical, chesty anxiety that I was not to experience again until I watched my own children walk along ledges or cross a busy road. What would happen to Liam among all those strong bodies? What would happen to his body? He was too young to understand you only got one. Fortunately, it was only twenty minutes or so before he came back out of the crowd and grasped his beer.

'Liam,' I said, 'I love you. You have to promise me to always use a condom and never get AIDS.'

He snorted. 'Kate,' he said, 'I've had my little dance. We can go now.' And then he drank his beer, and we went out.

'Was it the right club?' I asked, steering him to the tube.

'Yeah,' he said. 'Thanks. I'll find it again.'

Akash's Play

We are a hundred miles from the pub in Essex. Liam is in Italy, hitched to a European aristocrat; Jane is Head of English in a school in Kent. We are in a school with thirty-two languages and no majority culture. My students still use 'gay' as a pejorative term, meaning weak or old-fashioned, but not often, and it has none of the bite of the newer coinage 'moist'. And now we have invented smart-phones, Facebook, Twitter, Grindr, and Tinder, and our sexual identity has gone to live there: glittering, flexible, self-conscious. Are we all 'fluid' now? Perhaps. It is common-place to proclaim oneself transsexual. And to actually be gay, especially if you are as pretty as Kristen Stewart, is positively fashionable. A couple of kids have even changed gender, a decision so deliciously of the moment, so furiously defended by righteous students against non-existent op-position from staff that I worry only that they won't feel the freedom to change back if they feel the need.

We are in the library, reading Akash's play. His hero, Hari, is coming out, which still seems to be a fairly big deal. In fact, Hari has been stuck at 'Mum, I've got something to tell you . . . I'm—' for the last fifteen drafts. Otherwise, the play, *Gods in Nepal*, is evolving rapidly. It started as a version of Tony Kushner's play about AIDS, *Angels in America*, with the Buddha and Ganesh wandering around a deconstructed country. Since then, Akash has read a load of Brecht, and it has become a metatheatrical production with shades of *Mother Courage*. On the stage, there are to be three visible levels. The gods are in the Gods, talking over everyone's heads in sonnets, while the higher-caste Nepalese people, including a nasty man and his wife, are stuck on a precarious middle tier, desperate trying to maintain themselves and their property against threats coming from the gods above, and also from the peasants below. Hari, a Nepalese boy living in England, arrives on a plane with his mother, who is also the nasty man's discarded concubine, and wanders all three levels, partly in pursuit of a gorgeous Nepalese peasant boy. At the end of the play, the gods, getting fed up with everyone, destroy all the tiers in an earthquake, and in the resulting chaos, Hari has a first kiss and loses his mother. At the very end, on the phone, he has to tell his mother something; he has to say: 'Mum, I'm . . .'

It ought to be easy. But then, Akash himself didn't actually say those words. He did not, himself, so much come out as bloom into a thousand petals. He was thirteen when he handed me his flagrant and exciting story 'Pastel Wings', and he handed his beloved German teacher a copy at the same time. Not that we were very surprised.

'We had you figured in Year 7,' I tell him now, as I have before. 'Me and Miss C.'

'Outrageous,' says Akash, as he always does. 'How very dare you.'

But in Year 7 he was in the habit of strolling the corridor

with a girl on either arm, chatting confidentially, and the Languages corridor was adorned with his fashion drawings: attenuated figures in exotic outfits, labelled with the German for leg, arm, and – because Akash always goes the extra mile – armpit and false eyelash.

'You were quite noticeable,' I tell him. 'And when you won the writing competition and we met the duchess, remember? And you said you'd rather have Meryl Streep? That was also a clue.'

We could also mention the Prince songs in the corridors, the photographs – it's not just the profile, Kate, you have to think *jawline* – the haircuts, the dancing. Akash can be as camp as Paul ever was, and as in love with the musical, though his tastes are more towards Sondheim.

But he has grown less so with each passing year, as if it has become less necessary to him. At sixteen, the age I met Paul, Akash is already a more sober person, with none of Paul's self-abbreviating, fugitive quality. If we take camp to be an act of travesty or comedy, a transgressive, theatrical statement of otherness, then it's a limited place to live, its acts necessarily brief, its best lines all replies. Kenneth Williams, say, had to live as a permanently camp person because of the times he lived in, and it's a tragedy that Paul, as late as the nineties, was driven to that same corner by Essex and its mores. For Akash, camp is only one of the many places he can live, travesty only a tiny part of his range; he writes plays and directs them, dances, paints, writes, and is one of the cleverest kids in the school, as intellectual and eccentric as Liam ever was, in fact, though a more flowery, plangent writer. But perhaps Liam's black humour, his razor-sharp observations, that swooping irony I liked so much, were also features of his isolation. Liam's sexuality meant he was undercover in hostile territory; he saw so much because he was on high alert.

Akash isn't isolated. Partly, this is because, like Paul, he is intensely socially aware and uses his camp, impossible-to-insult persona to make himself universally popular. He is all over the school prospectus, in every photograph, showing that jawline; in the corridor, he is always surrounded by friends, his hints about his sexuality and his pashes on impossible blond boys the subject of many giggles. But his friendship choices are never bounded by teen politics; if anything, it is the reverse: he seeks out all kinds of otherness and foreignness. He has a passion for languages; he speaks, besides German, his own Nepalese, passable Urdu, K-pop Korean, a smattering of Mandarin. Any child new to the school will be targeted by Akash – who are they? Where from? – and forced to divulge enough clues about their language for him to launch himself into it, grinning at his mistakes, clutching onto Indo-European and K-pop roots until he is surfing the waves of incomprehension with utter pleasure.

Akash joined my senior Poetry Group when he was just thirteen, and immediately homed in on the silent and gifted Jennifer. There should be no reason why a sixth-form girl like her should speak to a boy like him, except that he insisted on it and they were both of Asian heritage. He mobbed her with his charm; he begged to read her notebook; he tracked her home. It worked: she adopted him as a sort of little brother, and they remained devoted, and exchanged writing, for years. Conversely, when we go on a residential writing course he picks out the only child I was worried about to take under his wing. Amy is two years younger than him, desperately anxious and shy, a carer for her ill mother, and the only Afro-Caribbean girl on the trip, but after Akash has announced to everyone, frequently and loudly, that she is very special and so is her writing, we all fall into line, and not only that week: her whole school experience is transformed.

Akash's house of friendship is large, like his play, with many tiers. Partly, this is explained by his Nepalese heritage: in Akash's concept of family, there are many perches for big sisters and cousins. After Jennifer, several sixth-formers find this out too, and he walks the corridor with a bevy of them. There are also several spaces for aunts and uncles and kindly patrons, and here, his German teacher and I are comfortably installed. It's spacious up here, and very relaxed. Akash knows how to be given to, and how to thank without being cloying: a rare and graceful gift. Besides, I don't hold any of Akash's secrets; he has never told me anything I couldn't freely share with a roster of his teachers. When I look back on Liam's plight, I am glad of our times, and not just for him.

As Akash writes his play, our school is at its maximum diversity – barely 20 per cent of the kids white British, and the others not from a single minority but from dozens, from all over the globe. In Blastmuir and in Essex, the school was part of a monoglot white community that knew how to be itself; here, the school is a gathering point for one of the most mixed communities ever to function on the earth. Many of the students here come from religious homes which condemn homosexuality – Polish Catholic, Pakistani Muslim, or, like Akash, Nepalese Hindu – but that does not matter, because when they come to school, the children put those values to one side. These children are not raised, like the children of Essex, to be like their parents; they are raised to outdo them. This includes speaking English and succeeding inside English culture. Our school tells them a liberal attitude to sexual identity is part of being British. Akash shows them, in his vivid personality and many triumphs, that it can be part of succeeding, too.

At least, in school. Akash's persona here – socialite, dramaturge, de facto Head Boy – is different from his Nepalese identity. His Nepalese community all gained their British passports through soldiering; they are Gurkhas. As such, they are all warrior caste and very ambitious for their children. In this community, Akash has dubious status. It isn't the clothes, the selfies, the elaborate haircuts – there are places for all that in his well-worn Hinduism. And he has the correct caste name – Guraung. But he does not have a father, just a lower-caste single mother, who is, like Hari's mother in the play, effectively his father's discarded concubine. She is barely fifteen years older than he is. In school, Akash is out and proud; at home, he does not have the words to even begin to explain to his mother what he is. Homosexuality is illegal in Nepal. All the good words for it are in English. His mother does not speak that language.

And this is the grit in Akash's pearl, the Kryptonite in his Superkid cave. His brilliance, his kindness, and perception, and anxiety, all go back to his mother to whom he is devoted, to whom he is brother, father, son; and to his dual identity, Nepalese and English. One day, he will have to explain that he is gay, and that is an English identity. In his play, it is after the earthquake, after his mother thinks he's dead, and on the phone, and still, he can't say it. Mum, he says, Mum, I'm . . . This is the fifteenth draft. These are the only words that have never been changed.

Mum, Mum, I'm . . .

Nepalese? I suggest, and Akash laughs his head off, like the kid he still is.

Javel's Rose and Emmanuel's Trousers

I watched Bill Forsyth's 1981 film *Gregory's Girl* recently. Gregory is just a little older than I am, and his school looks as outdated as my memories of Blastmuir High: concrete panels and big windows, long corridors with hefty fire doors, miles of bleak playing field. Inside, though, the wacky, febrile atmosphere Forsyth creates is still warmly recognizable as school. The earnest PE teacher, the baking-obsessed Steve, the melancholy penguin that flip-flops down the corridors to no one's surprise: I still know them. Gregory seems ahead of his time, what with his gay best friend, super-assertive wee sister, and adoration of the sporty Dorothy; as he himself says, 'Modern girls, modern boys, it's tremendous.'

Just one thing jars in Bill Forsyth's vision, but it jars hard: the wildly outdated, over-intimate, casually sexual-ized relationships of the teachers to the pupils – the two moustached English teachers giggling over the juicy girls who write them poems; the middle-aged woman inviting the former pupil turned window cleaner to 'come up and see me sometime'; the sweet PE teacher showing Dorothy how to catch a ball with her bum, one to one, alone in the changing room. All unimaginable now, but it was normal then, just as it was normal, a decade later in Essex, for the teachers to go to the pub at the end of the year with the Year 13s. I did that. And I took Liam to that club. I went to the pub with teachers myself as a sixth-former, and no harm came of it; nevertheless, I'm shocked now. Mores around sex have changed in schools in the last thirty years; changed unrecognizably, and, mostly, for the better.

My friend M definitely thinks so. She went to a *Gregory's Girl* comprehensive in the nineties and ran away south when she was only sixteen. She agrees, no one more strongly, that the sexist and homophobic attitudes of that school and that time held her back academically and emotionally, and injured her gay brother almost irrevocably. Now, after many adventures and a late degree, she teaches in a big comprehensive in outer London, and, ironically for such a wild child, is extremely strict. Order is one of the things she feels she was deprived of as a child; intellectual stimulation is another. 'Why shouldn't they sit and listen?' she says of her pupils. 'I know so much more than them. And besides, I'm very interesting.'

She is. She is also very glamorous, with a tall, neatly turned figure, long legs always in shiny tights, and a mane of Scottish red hair. She has a fine, arch Scottish manner too, another thing she aims to teach: 'By Year 11, one's class should be more of an intellectual cocktail party,' she says. Judging by her phenomenal exam results, she very often achieves this. She is not very keen on admin, but despite herself has risen to Second in Department, in charge, among other things, of the student teacher interns; a job she does with typical vigour, alternately adoring and despising the new recruits, always demanding vast efforts from them, vast as her own.

Last year, M was sent two very promising, biddable student interns, both young women, whom she nicknamed 'The Stepford Misses' because they were so very coiffed and created such neat lesson plans. They were dull but no trouble, she told me at Christmas. Which was why it was surprising, this summer, to have her on the phone in tears. One of her Stepford interns had written to her expressing her concern about M's 'potentially abusive/inappropriate relationship with a student'. M had received this email at eleven thirty at night on a Sunday at the strung-out, overheated end of the summer term, and had responded, being M, with a volley of highly articulate abuse. She thought it would go away, but instead the matter had been referred to the Deputy Head, and M had been summoned to a meeting.

I probed a little further, and this was the 'potentially abusive/inappropriate relationship' in question: The intern was working with M's Year 11, a second set that M had domineered, pummelled, and loved into kids who got As and had English as a favourite subject. They all adored her. (Of course, said M.) Javel, a tall, handsome Jamaican boy, started to express this adoration by bringing her every day a red silk rose. M thanked him very much each time, then placed the rose in a vase on the windowsill, making a display for the whole class. The problem occurred when the intern came in one morning to take the register, and Javel explained, of the roses, 'I'm flirting with Miss M.'

'That's not abusive,' I said, flabbergasted, on the phone to M. 'That's not really flirting, either.'

'No,' said M.

'And the Deputy Head can't have thought so either,' I added.

'No,' said M, still sounding doom-laden. 'He was very polite to her, though. He went through it all point by point. Her emails, my emails.'

'Your Sunday night email?' I said.

'Yes.'

'Maybe,' I said carefully, 'maybe you shouldn't have called the Stepford intern a virgin.'

'Maybe not,' said M, and she giggled a little, but she still wasn't laughing in the proper M fashion, so I probed a bit more, and the story of the second Stepford intern tottered shabbily into the light.

The previous term, M had placed this student teacher in her Year 8: lovely keen little kiddies. Everything was going beautifully, even at the stage when the intern was left to teach alone. Then, suddenly, M was summoned to an urgent lunchtime meeting with the Deputy Head. The intern had gone home and was reporting assault from one of her pupils, but when M was given the name, she thought there must be a mistake, another older boy with the same name, elsewhere in the school. Because her Emmanuel was top of the class, the sweetest, swottiest boy imaginable, and one of those who, at thirteen, was still very small, still seemed to be a child.

But it was her Emmanuel, and this was the assault. At the end of the lesson, Emmanuel had stayed behind to talk to the intern about, she thought, homework. But instead, he said, 'Miss, I love you, I think about you all the time.' The intern had left the room at once and reported the incident to the Deputy Head. Then she left the school and was never able to return, because the event had 'triggered' a previous assault.

'But,' I said, baffled, 'he didn't touch her. And how scared can she have been? It's not like he was threatening her.'

'He had an erection,' said M. 'Visible in his trousers.' She snorted. 'It must have been a very small one. A tiny tent.'

And what happened next was . . . Emmanuel was excluded for three days for assault.

'Oh, the reintegration meeting was terrible,' said M. 'The intern didn't show up because she didn't want to be "triggered", Emmanuel's dad was in total denial, nothing happened at all, he kept saying. I think he's going to take him out of school.'

'Emmanuel?' I asked.

'Just destroyed. And me, I was, I was . . .'

'Very, very angry?' I suggested. 'With her?'

'Yeah,' said M. 'We were all very angry. The whole department, his form teacher, the Deputy Head really – he's a decent guy, he was only playing it by the book, doing what had to be done. Angry with her. The intern. None of us thought it should have happened. None of us knew what to do.'

'And,' I asked, 'do you think that's what made you so angry about Javel?'

'Oh,' said M, 'definitely. Because I could have cleared that up in two minutes, normally. That was nothing. Javel's quite big and grown-up. It was just a job lot of roses his uncle sold him. But Emmanuel . . . It was only love. Love happens. Poor kid. Poor little boy.'

Of course, love happens in school. Schools run on love. Love of her academic subjects and her pupils, and for the family of her school, is what gets M up every morning, what keeps her going all the way to parents' evening or to the late-night marking of books. M's love, like most teachers' love – even that of Gregory's PE teacher for his football team – is *agape*: the pure, parental strain. This word, like most philosophy and most Greek, has sadly disappeared from teacher training manuals.

So has *ludus*, and there is a lot of that sort of love in schools too. *Ludus* as in *ludicrous*: the fun, experimental, uncommitted kind of love. This is the sort that *Gregory's Girl* celebrates so well – the silly, kindly cheerfulness that sends Gregory on a wild goose chase with three girls, or his little friend on a trip to Caracas. Part of a school's job is to supply a safe setting for this kind of love: the school play, the supervised prom, the residential trip. Done properly, these occasions create happy memories for life and a million wedding videos; made safe, *Midsummer Night's Dream* dazzlements can be shed in the morning, like an ass's head.

And then, dangerously dancing among the *ludus* and the *agape*, because schools are huge buildings filled with hundreds of adolescents, is *eros*, physical love. Schools work to exclude this, quite properly, but always in the full and certain knowledge that they cannot wholly succeed. Some pupils, like Emmanuel and Javel, will always get the sorts of love mixed up: the teacher's job is to strive never to do so. The teacher who, for example, builds on the *ludus* of the school play to seduce its star, or the fun of the ski trip to snog a sixth-former, or who forgets their *agape* love to move in on a child who makes, like Emmanuel, a declaration, is committing a terrible crime. It is right that these crimes are now so much more often reported, but it is wrong for teachers to forget their duty to other sorts of love, and wrong to give love a bad name.

Javel probably did have some sort of erotic crush on Miss M, but he was making it into *ludus*, into play, each time he offered M a rose, and M was making it over into *agape* each time she accepted a flower and placed it in the vase as part of her lesson, part of her 'cocktail party', the love-filled, playful classroom that she had painstakingly created. When the first Stepford intern called that love down, of course M was outraged; the intern was ignoring her professional knowledge and delicacy, and also the principle that governs her life: her commitment to teacherly *agape*. There are painful racial prejudices at play here, too. Javel brought his gifts partly because he came from a courtly Jamaican tradition of respect for the teacher; but the intern was treating him, and imagining M to see him, more like a big, black sex object. Emmanuel's home was a strict, Christian,

African one, one where sex was absolutely taboo. To send Emmanuel back to such a home for sexualized behaviour was life-changing, school-destroying, for both boy and family.

M's response to Javel was exactly right. And the correct response to Emmanuel's declaration would have been to ignore the *eros* and respond with *agape*: to say it was lovely that he was enjoying English, and suggest he go swiftly to the library to find a new book, and to not look at all at his trousers. A teacher not capable of a sacrifice like this is not a teacher. To the pure all things are pure; to the teacher all love is *agape*. M knew that, and the new generation of teachers who come from a much more self-conscious sexual culture, one created in the age of the internet and the selfie, could do worse than to learn it.

About Exclusion

Kylie, Royar, and Simon

When my littlest child was three, he sat on my lap to read our new library book: *Borka: The Adventures of a Goose with No Feathers*. He listened contentedly as Borka was hatched with the eponymous genetic deficiency, smiled when she had a compensatory jumper knitted for her. But winter was coming, and migration, and you cannot fly in a woolly jumper, so, in a double-page spread, Borka's family flew away. At this, my son let out a scalded howl. He leapt from my knee and cast himself to the floor. *They left her behind*, he howled. *They left her behind.*

I tried to console him. I flipped forward in the book, told him how Borka gets a boyfriend and a boat ride and nice individual identity, she's the heroine, damn it, she gets a book to herself . . . But I could have wept myself, looking at the picture of the small goose and its ascending siblings. How had such a work been stacked in a public library, let alone warmly recommended for children? Had the author, publisher, librarians, all forgotten how it felt: the backs turned in a playground, the adults' coats moving off down the lane, the beat of wings overhead?

I remembered. I remember. When I was a child, as Frank O'Hara puts it in 'Autobiographia Literaria', 'I played by myself in a / corner of the schoolyard / all alone.' And was changed and marked for life, like all writers.

But I don't think it's just writers and artists who feel like this. Not to be *left behind*, never to be the one dressed differently, acting differently, feathered differently, never, never to be excluded: for children, that is a primary drive. It is connected to the inbuilt Darwinian drive to walk with your tribe, stay with your kind, and it is stronger in a seven-year-old than the fear of death.

Conversely, children will do anything to be included, anything from wearing school uniform to marching with political youth groups; anything from joining in the inter-house litter-pick to beating up their dearest friend. The time when you were cruellest, or when your schoolfellows were, probably has something to do with that need to be included, to have the right feathers – remember?

Schools remember. They run on the powerful forces of exclusion and inclusion, and always have; that is what houses, prefects, old boys, rugby clubs – and their converse, Goths and Columbine – are all about. Now we no longer hit children, in fact, exclusion is our central punishment, and comes in different sorts and under different names, regulated, as it needs to be, by the law: internal exclusion, fixed term exclusion, and the ultimate, permanent exclusion, or as teachers call it, rhyming pleasingly with pox, PEX. It's a verb: I PEX, you PEX him, he got PEXed.

As a teacher, and parent, I knew this. I also knew how exclusion from school correlates strongly with wider social exclusion, both for children and the adults they become. Nevertheless, when I looked up from *Borka* to find I was being offered a job in the Inclusion Unit of our local school, working for a new charity, my first thought was that the unit's name was funny because, like 'Mental Health' and 'Anger Management', it mostly meant the opposite. This was the Exclusion Unit, really: the place where they put the kids they threw out of classes because they couldn't contain them.

And who on earth, I wondered, would be excluded from *that* school, the one already at the bottom of the local pecking order, the one already filled with the socially excluded, with refugees and migrants? I thought I might like to find out. I thought I had had enough of sitting at home, like Frank O'Hara, writing my poems. I thought that the students in the unit, the Excluded, might be a glamorous crew, something like the kids in the movie *Freedom Writers*. I thought, I fear, that I could do them good.

Kylie's Baby

And so it happens that one morning in January, I make my way through dirty snow to a low, batten-boarded building at the edge of the school grounds. Inside, it's cosy, over-heated, smelling of toast, and here is Miss B, bustling towards me in a new, crackling dress: 'Miss! We're having a rough morning, how are you? Happy New Year!'

It's break time, and the girls are huddled round the heater, attempting to dry the ballet slippers in which they have walked to school. Anorexic Clarice has spread hands thin and veiny as leaves on the copper radiator cover. 'Ooh,' she murmurs to herself, like a grandmother, clutching her sweatshirt to her hollow chest. 'Ooh, I never did.'

Kylie begs as I pass, 'Miss, I've dropped my shoe, get it out for us?' She can't reach down the back because she is so tiny; her leopard-skin pump is a size three. And she can't get a ruler, and give the thing a poke, because such enterprise is beyond her.

I get the shoe out. The girls murmur, gratefully, complainingly, resettle themselves around the radiator. They are far from the multi-racial, glamorous kids I had pictured. They are all white, for a start, though most of the kids in the neighbouring school are brown, and none of them, except spooky, platinum Angel, who rarely turns up in any case, is pretty. It isn't their features; it's because they don't look well. Often, they don't even look young; Simon has premature wrinkles on his forehead, Dave a middle-aged belly. This morning, their skin papery from the cold and their dyed hair thrust in clips, the girls could be middle-aged too, mothers queuing defeated and harmless in the Co-op.

But they are not harmless. Each one of these kids has the power to end learning in any mainstream class at any time, and each of their powers, as always in a gathering of superheroes, is different. Gentle Tom, when asked to write, may put his head on the table and start to hum like a blue whale. Gigantic Dave, who is so quiet, mostly, careful of his outsize hands as puppies, can turn suddenly, terrifyingly violent. *Damage*, it says on his report. *Damage* of desks, chairs, doors, other kids. Kylie will ignore you, root through her extra-large handbag for lipstick and start putting it on as if she were a bus passenger and you a faraway stop. If you ask for her attention she may laugh in your face: outraged, astonished laughter, as if you'd requested a snog. Vikki will announce a disability at high pitch, like a train's hooter: *Them's scissors, I can't use scissors, I can't, Miss, too hard. Doesn't work well out of comfort zone* it says on Vikki's report sheet, but her comfort zone seems passing small.

The Excluded are particularly ruffled and exhausted this morning because Miss B has induced them to take the exam for a GCSE module in Science. Exams are not the Excluded's thing; they have long records in avoiding them (Simon), walking out of them (Vikki), sleeping in them (Kylie), and throwing chairs at them (Dave). For Tom, who is severely dyslexic, the paper was as terrifying as dropping off a cliff, and now he is collapsed in a corner, drawing a picture in biro of an unhappy small boy standing by a large teacher's desk. It's very good; I especially like the boy's meticulously foreshortened feet, twisting in dumb despair.

Dave is beside Tom, watching, glass-blue eyes vacant, head in those enormous hands. Simon is in a different corner, twitching over his iPod, pulling the headphones in and out of his ears. Vikki was late, she just can't help herself, and is still finishing the paper in the outer lobby under the eye of Mrs N, the kind and motherly teaching assistant. Every time Vikki sighs, or drops her fluffy pen, or starts drilling through the page with it, Mrs N meets her eye, and shakes her head. There is some doubt if Vikki will finish, as she never has before. Nevertheless, Miss B gets out the chocolate, to celebrate. After all, the rest took the exam. They all sat there, all through.

It's worth celebrating; according to the report sheets I was shown at the start of the project, the Excluded were scheduled to get Gs this year. Today, several of them will have reached C grades, and Simon, who is smart as paint, at least a B. This is down to Miss B; I have watched her teach Science, clear and exact and demanding. And watched her do a number of other things too: tackle Social Services over the phone; talk down Dave, determined to leave the IU and smash something; phone Vikki, in the Co-op buying fags, and persuade her, for the fiftieth time, that it is worth coming into school. Miss B's degree is in Psychology, though what she does for the Excluded is not theoretical, but cognitive and practical. She chivvies these unpromising children, chides them, cheers them. She mops up, phones up, bandages, sorts. She creates unbending routines. She endlessly produces toast. She is without stint, without limit, without grudge; she is utterly reliable. Patience is often thought to be a passive quality, but Miss B's is active, intellectual, passionate, and remarkable. And it works, this super-concentrated mothering: the Excluded's *comfort zone* has already grown, before my wondering eyes, to encompass scissors, paper, desks, the IU, some adults, me. This does seem to have a long-lasting effect, too. Most days, one of Miss B's graduates calls by, to tell her how they're doing in college or sixth form, to get a dose of her still-ready affirmation.

No, here in the IU it's me who does the Freudian stuff,

though that was hardly the original intention. I'm supposed to be leading a writing project, one with notebooks, and an internal e-group for editing fiction in progress. What they do want to do, with almost embarrassing simplicity, is write about themselves, and whatever Hilary Swank ideas I may have had at the start, this makes me uneasy. I am nervous of the moments of revelation. I feel unqualified; I feel embarrassed; I become aware of my greedy, writerly curiosity.

Nevertheless, here they are, and here am I, and there is no point in studying the sonnet, here. So, after a few duff sessions, we have come up with a system. I read them something aloud – they love, like little children, to be read to – and in the brief peace afterwards, they write things down; a version of what we've read, usually, something in a strong rhetorical frame that makes their hesitant thoughts sound grand and fine. Then Miss B and I gather up the scribbles and file them, affirming as loudly and firmly as possible as we go. We have to do this; otherwise, they will destroy their work, because all of them, for all their bluster, have low self-esteem. In the same way that they cannot sit exams, get to school on time, or shift from radiators, the Excluded are unable to redraft their own work because that would involve reading it, and, as they wrote it, they know it is not worth doing so. So, each week I type and arrange their pieces nicely on an A3 sheet. I take their names off. That way, when we read them, they can see past their own unworthiness, and notice that their work is good.

Today, the story is a Julie Orringer one called 'Note to

Sixth-Grade Self'. It's quite long, which will be restful for
them after that exam, and I think they'll like the setting too – in America, in a high school, where soap opera
teenage-hood happens. We'll listen to the story, and maybe
Simon will tell us some more about his childhood, that
savage nearby hinterland full of dens and fires. Of all the
Excluded, Simon interests me most. He is so bright and
mercurial, and so full of stories

But Simon isn't talking today, let alone leaning back in
his chair and telling us spellbinding stories of arrest and
arson. He isn't in affirmation mood, either, when he urges
the others on in their work, weeps at their testimony, and
writes himself ringing prompts to resist 'peer pressure'
and to move on and get qualifications and a job. He has
dragged himself to the central table, but he is still plugging
the earphones in and out, dumping his head in his hands.
Eventually, he goes out to the lobby and sits with Mrs N.
Tom starts another drawing, asking dutiful permission
first. The others, though, are writing like mad, except the
ones who are crying, because I've really overdone it this
time. Julie Orringer hit a hell of a nerve, or maybe it was
Simon's head, or maybe even the exam, but something is
loose in the room, something dark.

Dave is writing to his ten-year-old, tortured, probably
autistic self, about to throw a chair at a teacher. 'Throw
harder,' he writes. 'Think about it. Aim.' This is light relief:
elsewhere, the Excluded are remembering being shut in
cupboards, knife attacks, sexual assaults, and over and
over, abuse by their parents; abuse which ranges from
simple neglect and abandonment, through complicated

excluding and scapegoating, all the way to sexual abuse and prostitution and outright criminal violence. The accounts have the poor spelling, incontinent exclamation marks, and the artless detail of truth: 'I slid down the stairs on my bum, so they wouldn't hear me.' 'You could see the blood on the carpets, in track marks like a car.' 'It was the big knife out the draw in the kitchen.' 'He was my mum's friend, I know him all my life.'

However unglamorous these kids, the stories on the crumpled bits of A4 are stark and clear as any Hollywood movie. Here, in black and white, is the liberal creed about children: no one is bad, though many are sad, and a few are mad. Dave acts like a cornered dog because he has been kicked like a dog; Vikki's comfort zone is small because she has been comforted so little. Kylie laughs at you when you ask her to be a normal girl because she knows she comes from a socially despised family. Clarice controls her world through starving her body because her body has been taken out of her control.

That children only do as they are done to, and generally less; that children can escape the legacy of their parents, and change: this is the founding myth of the IU, and, walking round the classroom, poring over writing, removing apostrophes, passing the tissues, I believe it. Certainly, nothing the Excluded have done, no bit of 'damage' to desk, carpet, or person, is anything compared to the damage done to them. For lack of something better to say, I repeat this to them. All of them are trying to do better, are doing better, are capable of kindness, too. As a group, they are strikingly nice – as Miss B often comments

– to each other, much more so than most children in their circumstances.

Kylie is still writing. This is unusual; normally, if she writes anything at all it is dashed off in a few lines. Today, she hands me a full A4 sheet of paper. 'Letter to my baby at sixteen weeks.' 'Young mom's are not slag's! There pregnancies are just as exciting as older mom's!' Ah. I scan the page. The abortion refused, the ultrasound picture framed . . . And is the father taking responsibility? 'He's in the lobby,' says Kylie, thumbing at Simon, slumped under his raincoat, murmuring to Mrs N, looking every one of his fifteen muddled years. 'He's being really good.'

I meet Miss B's eyes across the room. 'Miss!' I say, and, over Kylie's head, make the internationally understood hand signal of pregnancy.

'Miss,' she replies, and makes the international sign for utter despair.

I walk home, through slush which somehow seems much colder. I get under the duvet, worry that literature has had this result, put the radio on. *The World at One*. And here is the news about two young brothers from a Black Country town who attacked, tortured, and nearly killed two other boys, aged nine and eleven. Up in court today, sentenced. The boys, the most cursory of journalistic searches reveals, come from a family that has been workless since the pit closed, from violent and missing parents and grandparents, from a home without boundaries.

The poor we have always with us, as Jesus said, but now, in the first decade of the twenty-first century, we are beginning to focus on a particular sort of poor: families like the Black Country one, or the one shown in the TV series *Shameless*. Post-industrial families, thrown out of the traditional jobs that had both sustained them and enslaved them; caught in a cycle of poverty and deprivation; unable to find their way. Not the working classes any more, but non-working, the under-class: the Excluded.

Kylie's family, like the Black Country brothers' family, has been fatherless and workless for three generations, since not the pit but the car plant closed. She and her six siblings were born to a single, very young mother, and have several different fathers, none of whom currently lives with the family. Three of the six children are now mothers themselves, and all the babies live at home with the grand-mother. Kylie's baby will live there too: a third or perhaps fourth generation of fatherlessness and hopelessness, of desperately narrow horizons and the inability to get one's own shoe from behind the radiator. Should we – the state, the law – do something about this? If so, what, and how?

The debate on the radio is about how many chances Social Services had to intervene with the brothers' family, and why they failed. The call is for forcible fostering, compul-sory infant adoption. Perhaps that is what the Excluded's stories are begging for: someone to take them away before the thing with the knife, someone to get them out of that damn cupboard under the stairs, the one we find ourselves in, in the IU, session after session. Perhaps that is what would break the cycle. Compulsory adoption. Before they are three years old. At birth. *An earlier intervention.*

But the state hasn't intervened yet with Angel-the-rarely-present, due to have a baby at Easter with her much older boyfriend, so I cannot see that it will intervene with Kylie. Angel is neglected to the point that when she had a medical emergency before Christmas, only Miss B and Mrs N went up to see her at the hospital, and then they had to make a second run to bring her clean underwear, because her mother wouldn't do it. 'No pants,' said Miss B, making another note in another file, emailing another social worker. 'Can you imagine?' Angel is surely on drugs, even I can see that, and her boyfriend is probably her pimp, and she has written me only one piece in all this time, three lines: black burnt house / on the hill / dad.

And I can't think that the state ought to intervene with Kylie, either. Taking away a child is a desperate cruelty, an extreme punishment, and Kylie is not a criminal. Nor will she give the baby up willingly, because that takes either personal disaster or a sort of mass cultural shaming, the Magdalen Laundry, and we don't believe in that any more. As Kylie so movingly put it in her essay: *Young mom's are not slag's.*

In relation to Angel, Kylie is well set up, a good enough mother. And she seems entirely pleased with the pregnancy, whatever Miss B and I might think. And why not? Simon is definitely the pick of the IU. Meagre though her benefits will be, they will constitute a larger contribution to the family budget than any other she is capable of getting, certainly short term. And she doesn't do long term, because she has not been shown how. Aged only sixteen, she will join the adults of her family, with an income as good as her sisters'. She will meet all her family expectations as firmly as a surgeon's son getting his place at medical school;

most of us do not want more than that. And if she is conscious, as of course she is, that those expectations are different from those of the society around her, what of it? That will only make her feel more inadequate in the world, only turn her further in on her tribe.

Fathers, though, do not do so well in this set-up. So what about Simon, who, judging by his agony, already sees, far more clearly than Kylie, a longer future, and the needs of the child as a person. Volatile, tender Simon, so prone to self-hatred and guilt, so desperately badly fathered himself. Simon needs all his energy to save himself.

And, above all, what about the baby, Simon's baby, smart, perhaps, as paint? Where do we place his rights next to the rights of his parents, also children? Because, as Kylie says, *right now he is all perfect and nothing bad has happened to him*. And that must have been true of the Black Country brothers, once.

Royar's Firecracker

At the same time as I am working in the Inclusion Unit, I am also volunteering the odd morning at our local asylum centre, writing letters for Kurds, Albanians, Iraqis, or Tanzanians. I like to do this; it keeps me in touch with the world of refugees and migrants I came to know through my neighbour and nanny, Antigona, and offers me a world of stories.

Sometimes, though, I worry that Antigona has broken me into a permanent soft target; certainly Nesrin, a vigorous

Kurdish widow with a marvellous nose, latches on to me quickly. First, she gets me to write a council tax rebate letter for her, then to organize a long-distance funeral, then she spots me in Tesco, bursts into tears, and insists I read a letter from her son's school, which is not, thankfully, my school, right there and then.

Of course, I'm not supposed to do this; I'm out of hours. That is just the first of many difficulties. The second problem is that, after I do reply to Nesrin's letter for her, in Starbucks on my laptop, she insists on leaving her email password on the computer so that I can write the ensuing correspondence for her and *as* her, phoning her as I go. This appeals in some ways to my theatrical nature, but is even more work out of hours, and also strange and embarrassing and makes me feel I will be found out if I use too many semi-colons.

Much more difficult, though, is the fact that she is supporting her son in the dispute with his school with the irrational, exclaiming, melodramatic energy that perhaps only a Kurdish widow who grew up in a village with more scimitars than telephones could possibly muster, while I am, instinctively, on the teachers' side. I've met Royar: he is large, handsome, macho, and impatient, and I can all too easily imagine him lounging on the back row in my classroom, chewing, nudging his friends, disrupting my lessons. In compensation, the crime I am initially required to write about is at least a dashing one. Get this: following some sort of dispute, Royar dashed away from the Assistant Head into the road outside the school and – there are various excited descriptions of this from different witnesses, including the driver – ran *over the top* of a 4x4 as it idled at the lights, and then all the way to the other side of the busy road, where he waved, merrily, to an audience of awed and emulous Year 7s. He has a five-day exclusion for this, but it seems longer because it runs into half term. Afterwards, he may be permanently excluded.

Nesrin wants me to write and say that Royar walked away at the end of school because the bell had rung and he didn't hear the Assistant Head at all, and the 4x4 was trying to run him over, that's why he had to climb it, and he was waving to his friends just to say hello, but I really cannot see how any of this can work. Our Head would exclude permanently for this crime, no question. Damn it, I'd exclude him; I wouldn't want him running over cars in front of my eleven-year-old. No, the only possibility, it seems to me, is to apologize wildly and beg for a 'fresh start' at a neighbouring school. ('Fresh starts' are a regular exchange between state schools, but given, usually, *before* major trouble like this. 'Fresh starts' come to our school especially regularly from the more middle-class establishments, because we always have places, though the traffic is supposed to go both ways. Emails are sent: 'Tallulah has friendship group issues . . . Staff are asked to correct her quickly if she becomes obstructive in lessons.' Sighs are uttered. Sometimes it works. More often, it helps for a bit.)

But Nesrin, as a proud Kurd, refuses to beg, and so does Royar. We have a standoff in the asylum centre, which I lose. After they leave, taking advantage of the laptop arrangement and banking on Nesrin's poor English, I write the apology/begging letter anyway, then tell Nesrin I've done so over the phone. I think I know best. Royar is in Year 11; if he gets PEXed for this he may well have to finish the year in the council-run Behavioural Unit, and then he won't get any GCSEs.

But my letter doesn't work. Or does it? On the fifth day of the exclusion, Nesrin rings me in confusion. While she was out, Royar and his aunt were suddenly visited at home by a different assistant head. The aunt had let fly volumes of Kurdish abuse and 'the Asshead', as Miss T calls these unfortunate middle managers, had left abashedly, but not before she had given Royar the very strong impression that he was permanently excluded.

But he can't be, can he? You can't do it like that. Not without letters. Not without some sort of process. There is nothing on email. There has been nothing by post. I am roused and riled. I fire off an email to the school asking for clarification, then go and ask Miss B about the law. No, she says, you can't exclude like that, and she shows me the full exclusion process, laid out in a lever arch file. You need reports on the student, special needs assessment, care plans, parental meetings and agreements: a large number of chances, essentially, each one agreed by school, child, and carer. Only when they are all exhausted can a child be excluded. It is the work of years.

Royar, says Miss B, should have his own school file, which he is legally entitled to view at any time. Nesrin should ask for it, because it would clarify things. A file contains – and she shows me Simon's, open on her desk – reports and records of a student's entire time in school, including all the behavioural interactions and agreements.

Simon's notes are extensive, to the point where they have colour-coded file dividers, but he has never been an easy boy. Miss B also recommends an educational charity, which I ring up. They tell me, yes, I should definitely ask for the file, and the formal notice of Royar's exclusion, and for the school's behaviour policy. Armed with these, we could ask the school governors for an appeal against the exclusion. All of this, though, must be done quickly if Royar wants an education, because, unless he is formally excluded, he can't be funded to be educated anywhere else. He is a clever enough boy, though he has never applied himself. He wants to get enough GCSEs to join, God help us, the army.

So I ask for the file, I request the appeal (it takes hours; you definitely need a degree), but before I can get a reply, Nesrin phones up full of cheer. A kind person from the school has come round, not a teacher exactly, but a mentor, that's the word. A Christian one. My hackles go up; there are far too many people called 'mentor' in schools, and I am suspicious of Christian agendas. Royar is a Muslim, at least nominally. But Nesrin is pleased. The mentor is kind, she says. Yes, he is working with the school. Yes, Royar has met him before. And the mentor says that Royar can join a sport course with the city football club and qualify as a coach. He'll love that. They've signed the papers already.

I go back to Miss B, suspicious. So is she. Not all schools, she explains, keep files like hers. And then, when the school decides they can no longer contain a student like Royar, they hit difficulties; they haven't gone through all the right steps, they haven't exhausted all those care plans and parental agreements and fresh starts, so they can't legally exclude. She thinks this might be the case here. Royar's school is also under another sort of pressure: Ofsted are due to inspect soon, and they frown on exclusion because it's too easy to push out difficult students and pass them down the prestige ladder to the school at the bottom. In their last inspection, in fact, Royar's school was specifically told that they exclude too much. So, in order to avoid Ofsted scrutiny while also reaping the benefits of getting difficult students off your roll and out of your figures – and let's say it one more time: these kids are poison for results – lots of schools do what Royar's is doing: hide difficult pupils under the carpet, or rather under the legal grey area of 'alternative provision'. In this endeavour, informal volunteers such as the Christian 'mentor' can be very useful, and so can well-meant private schemes such as the sport one.

So can profiteering private centres run by untrained and unqualified gap-year students, actually, as Sir Michael Wilshaw expostulated as he prepared to leave office in November 2016. The sport scheme isn't like this; it is genuinely run not for profit, and by a church. It is still, however, not useful for Royar: a mobile classroom staffed by evangelical Christians and filled with, as Royar says, 'not being nasty or anything, but like really thick kids. Some of them can't write.' The course is not run by the city football club at all but just uses some facilities sometimes, and it leads to Level 2 BTEC: a worthless qualification next to the five GCSEs Royar was expected to get, not good enough for the army. Even leaving aside the daily offence of a Muslim boy being subjected to relentless Christian evangelizing – which, to be fair, seems the least of Royar's concerns – it won't do.

So I turn back to the school. Where is the notice of exclusion, please? Where is the behaviour policy and the file? It's been weeks. After much nagging, they send a letter, but no notice of exclusion. Royar, we're told, has agreed to 'alternative provision', and therefore there is no exclusion and no appeal to the governors. But what, I ask, about the visit from the Assistant Head, when Royar was told he was permanently excluded? The school has no record of this. I ring the educational charity, who tell me that if there are no documents this is informal exclusion and illegal, no matter what Royar has agreed to orally. Nesrin can ask simply for a hearing with the governors about this case – it doesn't need to be an appeal against exclusion. She should get on with it.

But Nesrin is completely lost, of course, in the confusion. Left to herself, she would never even have started this process; she would have let Royar drop out of the football course and out of view. Clearly, too, this is what the school and its social worker expected her to do; what the parents of illegally excluded children generally do, because they are no more up to the system than their children. Informal exclusion could, it occurs to me, be happening on a very wide scale in this school, and in other schools too. No one would know. No one would know about Royar if I hadn't met Nesrin in Tesco.

Finally, I receive Royar's file. In contrast to Miss B's neat, colour-coded sections, it is a mess: a hasty print-out of past offences, mostly recorded through staff emails to one another, mixed in with occasional social workers' reports and notes from counsellors. So careless is it that the printed-out emails are freely attached to print-outs of other, personal emails, recording for example the 'yummy cake' Royar's form teacher plans to share with Royar's counsellor, and the Head's secretary 'nipping out into the corridor' to settle his fate with the school social worker.

The form teacher likes the counsellor, it emerges from the print-outs, but I don't. I don't like her judgemental comments on Royar's sexist attitudes, his rudeness towards her. Why is there nothing of Royar's background, of what it means to be the only son of a widow, with the honour of a family on his shoulders in a country which doesn't know what honour means? One day, Royar compliments the counsellor on her blouse and she reports on him to his form teacher. She says it is sexual harassment.

I don't like the form teacher, either. He takes Royar to task over the blouse remark, and the boy responds with macho pride and a deep sense of betrayal that the counsellor would tell such tales. The form teacher encourages the counsellor to refuse to see Royar again. They agree together that they shouldn't have to put up with this. Now I hate them, the form teacher and the counsellor, eating their yummy cake. I hate the social worker more, though, lounging in the corridor, signing documents off unread for the Head's secretary. Why has she never told the counsellor where Royar comes from, that his family are refugees, victims of torture? Why has she never replied to any of Nesrin's phone calls? No doubt the calls were inarticulate and desperate – but isn't that, exactly, part of her job?

It's the firecrackers, though, that send me actually round the twist and into a state where I do very little except

Royar's case for a month. The firecrackers don't even exist. In the last week of October, firework season, Royar was body-searched for firecrackers. The form teacher had a very strong notion that Royar might have some in his socks. Which maybe he could. Maybe if there were firecrackers in my school, setting off fire alarms, causing a nuisance, maybe if there were an overgrown Kurdish boy in my class whom the counsellor won't see because she finds him too threatening, a boy who is bold and rude and always has other boys around him – maybe that's where I'd look too. Royar's socks. But the school had forgotten a simple thing about Royar, the thing that wasn't in his file, the thing the social worker hadn't said, the thing the counsellor hadn't got to: Royar was from Kurdistan. In his childhood, he had been body-searched by soldiers who took his father away and later killed him. I don't know if Royar knew that body searches 'triggered' him; maybe he just found out that day, the day he ran away from the Assistant Head, and climbed the 4x4, and ruined his life.

I now understand why the helpful charity's Informal Exclusion casebook is mostly made up of the middle-class parents of kids with special needs: you need to be articulate, connected, and empowered to push through this legal morass. Well, I decide, Nesrin, voiced by me, shall become the most articulate Kurdish widow ever to hit the UK education system. I lose all inhibition about my semi-colons. I complain, in fine and biting terms, to the social worker about the nipping-into-the-corridor decision and copy my complaint in to everyone I can find on the council website. I receive by return a letter from her boss, asking, in effect, for more complaints. The boss, clearly, has been concerned about this lazy and collusive person for some time, but has been handicapped by the same thing that prevents so much action against informal exclusion: a lack of good clear evidence from articulate people capable of writing down the date. The suddenly fluent Nesrin sends the boss a bunch more complaints and gets the social worker fired; it's a pleasure and a gift.

I scythe on with my appeal to the governors. It's not about firecrackers, or yummy cake, or even evangelical Christianity, though I am sorely tempted on all counts. None of these things is needed; I simply have to point out to the governors that if you are going to exclude someone you have to do it by the book, and the school failed to do so. The only real difficulty is getting this statement through the many bureaucratic obstructions that the Head's secretary, who is also the clerk to the governors, puts up. It takes weeks, deep into January, to get to the meeting, by which time Royar has not had any education for nearly a term of Year 11.

Even when we win, as we do in less than half an hour, the school malingers. They refuse to make arrangements to readmit Royar, refuse to find him a form teacher, a reasonable timetable, until three weeks after February half term. This leaves him just a few weeks to catch up on his GCSEs, hard for the best student, which Royar is not. In fact, now I stop fighting, and turn to look at him, I see I may have done him no good at all. The lad who could never be kept at home, who played football and basketball at all hours, has morphed to a heap of depression who spends most of his time in bed. Exclusion has already had its chemical effect, even on a boy who hated school.

Nesrin turfs him out. He goes back to school: back to the hated form teacher; to the counsellor who thinks he's a pervert; the schoolfellows who used to have him as a hero, among whom he has now lost his place. He bows his shoulders for all of three days, then, in a return to Kurdish scimitar form, gets into a row over the late register and calls yet another assistant head, his third, a cow. Royar's file, thanks to all my interference, is more organized now, and he can be, and is, moved swiftly to permanent exclusion, and then to the council Behavioural Unit. His school doesn't have an Inclusion Unit, and from my seat in the asylum centre, gazing into Nesrin's beaten, bewildered face, that looks like the only possible place for Royar and his large and rag-tag ilk.

Simon's Child

At Easter, things are looking good in the IU. Tom has secured an apprenticeship and is a different boy: pink, straight-backed, early in every morning to work on his spelling. Vikki has a college place too, to study hairdressing, and she has fallen in love with Dave. It's taken years off both of them; Vikki has lost at least a stone and taken to bleaching and tonging her hair into dolly ringlets. Dave is flushed, tender, follows her around slack-jawed, stretching out a finger sometimes to touch her waist or a tinder-y curl. Kylie has grown a pregnancy bump the size of herself and slip-slops in, in her leopard-skin flats, more and more rarely, but Clarice, in compensation, has gained weight and is more or less back in mainstream class. And we have written a book, finest parts by Simon.

I am just organizing a little reading with local dignitaries when I go into school to find Simon not there and the Excluded in muddled, mutinous form. Our rehearsal goes very badly, and afterwards, Miss B and Mrs N beckon me aside to tell me Simon may not be able to make it to the reading, either, because he has been excluded. A week ago, Kylie told Simon the baby wasn't his after all, but another boyfriend's, and Simon went into a complicated spin that resulted in his bringing his hunting knife to school. A teacher spotted it, he refused to hand it over, he ran away, and got up the tree. 'Our tree?' I ask. The IU tree. Where Vikki goes to smoke. A big, bushy beech. 'He went up our tree with the knife?'

'Yup.' Miss B allows herself one snort. 'Isn't funny really,' she says, 'but there was such a fuss. We had to evacuate – they were going to evacuate the whole school. They'd called the police.'

'What did you do?'

'I went up there.'

'You did? The tree?'

'My knees won't let me,' says Mrs N, which wasn't what I'd meant. Going up the tree is very unlike Miss B, actually, because it is such a personal, irregular thing to do. Miss B usually plays it by the book.

'I couldn't think what else to do,' says Miss B defensively. 'And anyway, he came down.'

But to exclusion. Permanent exclusion. The record of the colour-coded file, so carefully kept by Miss B, clearly says where Simon is at, and it reads: Last Legal Chance. In bringing a knife to school, he has blown it.

We all realize, in the next weeks, how much we turned to Simon, how alive he was, the quick thing in the slow room. And how kind, too. He'd romanced us all, drawn us all into the story he was telling this year, which was about reform, a new life. Turnaround: an inspiring story. I needed that story too; and now Simon and Royar will both do their GCSEs in isolation, unsupported. Neither will do well.

But I ask Simon to come to the poetry reading anyway, personally, on his own account, as a free sixteen-year-old individual, not a representative of the school. And he turns up, stands swinging on his toes in the gilt-wood lobby of the city hall, wrinkling his elderly forehead, looking, honestly, as if he has come to mend the drains. Vikki and Dave flutter round him, Tom stands adoringly by his side, and they are all pleased as punch with the book. Then we go into the reading room: a handsome formal hall, set out with a low platform and light padded chairs, the kind they set out for weddings, and Simon sits down and weeps and says he will go no further.

'Simon,' I say, 'are you really not scared of knives but totally scared of a bunch of posh chairs?'

And he grins and says, 'It's what you're used to, Kate, ennit,' and consents to stagger onto the platform. He reads, and is a huge, huge, helium-and-champagne success, and we all find ourselves asked to a reception with a famous author where Simon deals with everyone with grace and aplomb, directing all compliments to Miss B – you don't know what she has to put up with – and me. When I go over to him, he grins over his plate of olive hummus and quails' eggs and says: 'I'm glad I'm not posh really. You have to eat terrible food.' And then I don't see him again for seven years.

Over those seven years, I meet all the girls from the IU again. Each is in a crowded, female place – the beautician's, the nail bar, Primark, the doctor's, the nursery school, the drop-in centre, the library – but I recognize each one without difficulty. Beside them, each has a baby. Teen mothers, living on benefits, mostly alone. In the noughties and the teens, a word is coined for them: *pram face*. The country turns against *pram face* in those years; efforts are made to speed up compulsory adoption, benefits are slashed, the *Daily Mail* monsters them regularly. In response, the teen pregnancy rate falls and the adoption rate goes up, but not by much. The problem Kylie presented in the IU continues to be a common and insoluble one.

Before I worked in the IU I disbelieved in *pram face*. That is, I knew teenagers had babies and also saw them leave schools in which I worked, but I did not believe that any one of them had done it as a choice. But all the IU girls did; they all got pregnant at least semi-deliberately and all the people I know who work closely with girls like this are also aware of pregnancy as a frequent and almost inevitable happening.

The IU girls did it to contribute to the family home, to be like their families, or because even six months in the council mother-and-baby unit as you waited for a flat was better than living in an unhappy home. They did it because they didn't know anyone who had done it differently, and middle-class choices such as university seemed completely unreal. They did it because they weren't willing to reject everything about their own upbringing, especially when people from different backgrounds had not been helpful to them. They did it because they wanted someone to love, and because they believed, as we all do, that they could make a better job of it than their own mothers. They did it because it was the only route to a bit of independence and status realistically available to them. They did it because they weren't stupid, not because they were.

And so did Royar, come to think of it. Nesrin fills me in eight years on. He hasn't joined the army. He hasn't held down a job. But he has two children with the same, much older mother, and Nesrin likes them.

Seven years later, I meet Simon again. I am in the line for the outdoor swimming pool; he is on his way out, a roll-up cigarette tucked in his teeth, his belly more middle-aged and his forehead more wrinkled than ever. He is walking a pushchair full of damp three-year-old and has a bigger child in hand. He seems pleased to see me. We talk about Miss B, then he says, indicating the toddler, 'This one's mine.'

'Where's the mum?' I ask.

'At home,' he says. 'You know her. Kylie. I'm still with her.' He has a twinkle in his eye, a knowing grin. Simon, who always had my do-gooding measure. 'That one,' he says, indicating the older child, by now halfway up a tree, 'he's not mine, but I've brought him up because he needs a dad.'

So this is Simon's baby. The baby of the long-ago cold morning in the IU. He looks fine, koala-clinging to his branch in shorts and T-shirt. He looks like any six-year-old. Any kid.

'Well done,' I say, sincerely.

'I couldn't leave him behind,' he says, 'could I?'

Miss B and I discuss it over coffee. She is getting married and I am to read a poem, but we brush pass that, as we always do, to talk about the IU, about that year. About what happened, and what was the good?

Our girls, says Miss B, mostly had their babies at eighteen and twenty, not sixteen. That's not turnaround, but it is something. It's better than fifteen and sixteen. And it is a most intractable problem, the Kylie problem. David Cameron, for instance, found this out when his 'troubled families' initiative collapsed, having spent a billion pounds and helped just 1,600 people into work.

'But lots of those families,' says Miss B, 'probably did better than they might. And the IU kids did do better than they might, much better. It just doesn't show up well on data.'

Simon is working in a bar, which is probably not anywhere near realizing his very considerable potential. So how do we reckon it up, the amount of love that he is managing to give to Kylie's baby, the loss it may have taken from his own young life, against the slowing it might cause in the spiral of deprivation, the speed at which the koala-child might end up in the IU? As for where that love came from, or the extent to which the year in the IU may have helped release it, or what was passed to Simon the day Miss B so uncharacteristically climbed the tree – who can say?

'I think it's huge,' I say to Miss B. 'I think it was a great thing, what you did in the IU. One of the best things I've ever seen.'

'Yes,' says Miss B. 'But I still wish I'd written it down. At the time. Got a record of it – a flipping MA or something. Something to show.'

But she was too busy with the actual good she was doing, so I have written this down instead.

About Nations, Papers, and Where We Belong

Shakila, Aadil, and Me

Lucky, this point in time and space
Is chosen as my working-place
W. H. AUDEN

My multicultural school – the one I teach in, the one my children go to – is the opposite of exclusive. Our town, like many in the south-east of England, has had huge influxes of migrants in the last twenty years – from the British Commonwealth, from the EU, and, most recently, from the crisis across the Middle East – and now our school includes, it seems, the whole world: students from Nepal and Brazil, Somalia and Lithuania, Portugal and the Philippines, Afghanistan and Australia, and everywhere in between. Pakistani and white British students make up substantial minorities, but there is no majority group.

This makes for innumerable cross-race friendships and for a particularly respectful atmosphere, a careful, decorous gentleness that comes from no one knowing quite what's what, from everyone being dependent on the kindness of strangers. It makes for beautiful scenes: a row of girls under the willow tree, their skin colours varying from black

Somali to white Polish with every shade of brown in between, laughing and gossiping together; a boy called Mohammed from Syria throwing the basketball to a boy from Brazil and shouting his name – 'Jesus, Jesus! Catch!'; our motley choir, representing all the nations of the globe, singing 'All You Need Is Love'; Jonathon, six foot five inches tall with a slow, resonant African accent, concluding the vote of thanks at a speaking competition with the words, 'And I wish to thank too this school for making me welcome and giving me shelter. Truly, you are kind in this country. Hand on heart' – and his hand was on his heart – 'I am thankful for this school in this country.'

Hand on heart, I am thankful too. But a school full of migrants, refugees, and difference also throws up questions about nations and belonging, and these are some of them.

Shakila's Head

It's Sports Day, and Shakila slips from the shade behind the library, blinking in the sun. 'Miss!'

I wonder again what Shakila does to her hijab, and why it seems to sit fuller and higher than the other girls' – a Mother Superior hijab, or one from a Vermeer. It can't be starched. Maybe it's draped over twisted horns of hair, like Carrie Fisher's in *Star Wars*. That would go with her furry eyebrows, her slanting, sparking black eyes, her general, Mongolian ferocity.

'Miss!' cries Shakila. 'I won the 400 metres!'

'You did? Isn't it Ramadan? Aren't you fasting?'

Shakila nods. 'I still won. And Miss! I'm coming to Poetry Group. After the hurdles. Here. Poem.'

She hands me a sheet of A4, and dashes back onto the playing field. It is twenty-eight degrees and getting hotter. Under her rugby shirt and long trousers, Shakila grows thin.

The poem, though, is very fine: a variation on a theme I gave the group last week, contrasting the morning *adhan* from the mosque in her native Afghanistan with the morning alarm of her new life in England. I'm more interested, though, in the writing on the other side of the sheet, which she has crossed out with a single line so the whole text is still visible and begging to be read. It's about a man sweating, and a scarf and a backpack and suspicious minds – so when, because of Sports Day, just Lily, Priya, and Shakila turn up to Poetry Group, I ask her about it.

'Oh,' she says, 'I was trying to write, you know, about terrorists.'

'What about terrorists?'

'But I couldn't make it work. Miss! It was too hard.'

'Terrorists here? In this country?'

I'm assuming the poem is a protest against suspicion of Muslims in Britain. I'm aware there is a group of Afghans in the neighbourhood now. The local cafe has a new name and a map of Afghanistan on the wall, and an invitation to order a whole sheep, twenty-four hours in advance. I got into a discussion with the cook about the poet Rumi. He looked just like Shakila, come to think of it, so maybe—

'No, Miss,' says Shakila, eyes snapping, ivory fingers blossoming in scorn. 'In England? There are no terrorists in England.'

'She's from Afghanistan,' says Lily, 'she means the Taliban.'

Lily is an alternative type, a Goth with heavy eyeliner who always knocks about with the black girls; nevertheless, I assume this is a white stereotype, and I am about to correct her when Shakila nods, more vehement than ever.

'Miss! I am Hazara people.'

'Like *The Kite Runner*,' says Lily, glancing at me smugly.

'I don't know,' says Shakila.

'It's a book,' I say, 'about Afghanistan. It's on the A Level, isn't it, Lily?'

'The Taliban,' says Shakila, 'hate us. When my mum went to get our visa, Miss, the bus was bombed – not her bus, but the one in front. Miss! I thought she would never come home.'

'But,' says Lily, 'I thought you was Muslim?' She offers me a Monster Munch. Usually, at Poetry Group, Shakila brings us cherries and strawberries, shining like the roses in her cheeks. She and Priya are pale today.

'I am Muslim,' says Shakila, 'I am Shia.'

'What's that?' asks Lily. I raise an eyebrow. Clearly, this wasn't in *The Kite Runner*.

'A different kind of Muslim,' I supply. 'Like Protestant and Catholic.'

'The Taliban hate the Shia,' says Shakila flatly. 'They kill us, all the time.'

Priya leans across the table. Her hijab is soft, striped, and biblical like in a nativity play, her teeth in braces, her face, as so often, full of delicate feeling. She is from Bangladesh, originally: a Sunni.

'Miss!' she says, but she is talking to Shakila. 'When I found out about that, when I learned that there are other kinds of Muslim, I didn't believe it. I said to my teacher in the mosque, this is not true, how can this be?'

'There is only one Koran,' says Shakila. 'There is only one Allah.'

Priya says: 'Miss! Don't laugh. When I was a little girl I thought the television was true. I mean, the black and white. I thought the past was black and white, Miss, I thought England was black and white. When I found out about Shia and Sunni, it was like that for me – I mean, when I found I was wrong.'

'You should write that down,' says Lily, 'this is Poetry Group. How old was you when you came here, Priya?'

'Six.'

'Me, I was fourteen,' says Shakila.

'Sunni, Shia, there is no difference really,' says Priya. 'Just – some prayers. Wait – do you whip yourselves?'

'No!' snorts Shakila. 'I mean, not really. It is a – thingy. A symbol.' She leans her hijab to Priya's hijab, puts her hands across the table. 'You know,' she says, 'in my country, they caught this terrorist, this bomber, they put him on television, he said he was doing it for the Taliban, but he didn't know anything, he did not know –' and she breaks into Arabic, sharp and triumphant – 'As-salamu alaikum.'

'Wa alaikumus-salam wa rahmatullah,' chimes in Priya, and both girls bow their heads.

'What's that?' asks Lily, and Shakila gazes at her.

'A salutation,' she says, 'a Muslim says it to a Muslim. Everyone knows that.'

'Except the Taliban fighter didn't know it,' I say. 'Or not with a gun to his head.'

'But,' says Lily, 'this bloke, the Taliban bloke on the telly, was he the same as in this poem?'

'No,' says Shakila, 'this was another one.'

Priya raises her head. 'How can a Muslim hate another Muslim? Miss! It is terrible, Miss.'

'A real terrorist?' says Lily. 'In your poem? Like, you met him?'

'Yes!' says Shakila. 'I saw him on the street – in the market – and I had this feeling, he is wrong. He is sweating, he wears all these clothes . . .'

'What clothes?'

'Like, you know, jacket, big thingy. Scarf, big trousers. It is hot, it is summer – I had a feeling, run away, run away from this guy. I catch my friend's hand. We run.'

'Yes,' says Lily, 'but was he real? A real terrorist?'

'Yes,' says Shakila, 'real. I ran, I screamed, I ran, everyone ran. There was an explosion. I was hiding, behind a thingy. Wall. He was in a bomb. He exploded. You heard it. Boom.'

And then the bell rings for a long time, and we flinch from its noise.

Priya says, 'You need a frame. For your poem. Miss. Give her a frame.'

A frame. They have learned my mantra. A frame, I say every week. Try this poem-shape, this form, this bit of rhetoric, this frame. Never: tell me about . . . Certainly not: unload your trauma. And still, they tell me these terrible things.

'Yes,' says Shakila, 'a frame. How shall I say it, Miss?'

I haven't the slightest idea. Shakila folds her hands on her bag, waits.

'That,' says Lily, 'was a really good discussion. I reckon we should have filmed it. Like for RE? I have to go.'

And she goes. So does Priya, leaving me to search my mind for the right frame for a poem about recognizing a terrorist in the market place and then running away.

Shakila says, 'Miss! You know, bombs. Miss, the worst thing is, they cut you. They cut off bits of you, Miss, like your feet, your leg! And when the bomb goes off, Miss, those . . . thingies?'

'Body parts?' I suggest, automatically.

'Yes!' Shakila's eyes brighten as they do when she sights a really fine piece of vocabulary. 'Body parts. Body parts, they land in the town around.'

'Did that happen in that bomb?' I ask. 'The bomb in your poem. Did you see that?'

'Miss,' she says, 'there was a head. A whole head.'

'His head?' I ask. 'The terrorist's?'

'Just,' she says, 'you know, a head.'

'Right,' I say. I look at the sunlight coming in the slats of the blinds and I suggest that the interrogative mood might be good for poems like this, and short lines probably, and regular stanzas. A ballad, perhaps, or a set of instructions. How to recognize a terrorist. Shakila says she will send me the poem, by email.

And she leaves. I sit and stare, listen to the roar of the children finding their classrooms, the silence as the doors close and the register is taken. This is an orderly school, I remind myself. A just one. A safe one. As Lily said, it is beautiful to see Shakila and Priya extend hands across the table. More people should know.

Then I think I will go to the staffroom and find someone to tell. There will be someone there, someone to listen and to counter with some equally horrifying tale, and we will rehearse all the interventions available, all the help school extends, which is good help, the best available anywhere, the best anyone can do. We will remind each other this is why we work here, why our school does so well. Our multi-cultural intake, our refugee pupils, so motivated, so very often brilliant, so, in the modern parlance, vibrant.

But it won't do any good. Here in my ears is the sound of a bomb, a homemade one, a glass and fertilizer one, in a small town in Afghanistan, and it sounds like the school bell. And here on the desk, disguised as a sheet of A4 paper, is a head cut off at the neck, its eyes shut, its bloodstains minimal, its skin greenish, like John the Baptist on a plate. Shakila's head, in its elaborate hijab, for how else am I to picture the Hazara people – Persian speakers, lovers of the poet Rumi, eaters of apricots, guardians of the Buddhas of Bamiyan – other than as my dear, my swift-running Shakila? Does she feel the lighter of it, I wonder, now it is me who has to carry the head home? Or will it be equally heavy, however often it is passed, just as much a head? Well, we can find out. Shakila's head: the weight of it, the warmth, the cheekbones, the brains. Here you are. Catch.

Aadil's Blood

Aadil is supposed to be helping on Open Evening, but he has arrived late with a bleeding nose. This is not picturesque, so I am hiding him in the empty staffroom and handing him cotton wool and paper towels from the medical bay. I am also trying to work out if he has been in a fight. I can't quite believe he has. Aadil always seems so grand: a tall Somali boy with a deep, African voice, and the almost aristocratically calm manner that sometimes goes with being extremely good-looking.

'I hit him first,' he says, before I can ask.

'Who?' I ask.

'Cumar,' he says.

'Cumar? You hit Cumar?' Now I'm really baffled. Cumar, as far as I am concerned, is super-nice; not as spectacularly clever as Aadil, perhaps, but bright and helpful and always opening doors for you.

'I thought you guys were from the same country?' I say.

Aadil sighs. Then he looks at me: a long appraising look.

'Is that how we look to you, Miss?' he says. 'Really?'

I think again. Cumar is long and slender as many of the Somali kids are, with a thin nose, narrow skull, and very dark, almost black skin. Aadil is more muscular and square-set, with chocolate-coloured skin, a broad-based nose, and rounded head. Very different, now I think about it. About as widely different, in fact, as I, with my Nordic height and Celtic colouring, am from a petite, olive-skinned, Mediterranean woman.

'Aren't you both Somali?' I ask. 'You told me you were Somali.'

'Miss,' said Aadil, 'I'm mixed. Like . . . Kenya–Somali mix. My mum and dad, they're from different . . .' He hesitates. He won't say the word 'tribe'; we've talked about that.

'They're from different groups. It's all mixed up, there, Somali and Kenyan? My mum – she looks like me. My brothers – they look like my dad. They look like Cumar. I look different. I look Kenyan. Cumar says I look Kenyan.' And his nose starts bleeding again and he reaches for the paper towel.

'If you're Kenyan don't you get asylum?' I ask.

Inside the paper towel, Aadil shakes his head.

'What about your story?' I ask, because Aadil has written me a beautiful memoir of witnessing and escaping Kenyan government violence as a four-year-old.

Aadil raises his head. 'Miss! That's all true.'

I know, instinctively, that it is. Of course it is. People on every border, deep into every country, are mixed heritage. The Kenyan border will be no different.

'Is Cumar from the border too?' I ask.

'Yes,' he says, 'Somali–Kenya border. Like me.'

So Cumar has identified Aadil, because he looks different, with his family's persecutors, who were Kenyan-looking. Probably, he hates Aadil more because he is so close to him, because they ought to be friends. I think for a minute, proceed carefully. I know that Aadil's papers, like those of so many of my students, are still in process.

'Are you worried,' I ask, 'that you might not get your papers if they think you're Kenyan?'

Aadil takes a long time to reply. His shoulders are shaking. At last he says: 'I'm worried my whole family won't get their papers if they think I look Kenyan.'

I can't pat his back; he's a boy. I look at the heaving paper towel. I rack my brains for something comforting to say.

At last I try: 'Look, don't worry too much. Cumar, he's totally not the British government, you know. People like me, that's who's in government. And what did I just show you? You look Somali to me. I've got no idea. Most of us – white people, English people – you look the same to us. We've got no idea.'

Aadil has the grace to put down the towel, and to smile.

My Papers

One of the things Aadil and Shakila teach me is how white I am. To these young refugees, or to the son of a Lithuanian hospital porter or the daughter of a Bengali warehouse worker, I am a super-empowered, incredibly lucky member of the world's ruling class; someone whose 'papers' – the visa, passport, work permit, the possession or lack of which very often dominates their family destiny – are perfect, wholly intact. They sum it up in one word: 'English', and I never correct them.

But I am Scottish, really, not English. Scottish by birth and Scottish by upbringing: a tiny difference which has had a surprisingly strong impact on my sense of self. Sometimes, too, talking to kids about the byzantine workings of the Home Office, I remember my own applications for 'papers'. Because the fact is, mine are not perfect, and I did not emigrate from Scotland; I was asked to leave. This is my story.

I went to school in Glasgow and then in Edinburgh in two almost entirely white schools, monocultures, like

Blastmuir High School. The effect of this seemed to be to highlight small differences: for example, I was white and Scottish born, but because I had an English father, and an Irish (Catholic) name, I was often counted among my peers as English. When I was little, I worried about this a good deal, and especially about my voice which was deemed to be very English indeed. I dreaded opening my mouth in front of new people, and often tried to avoid talking altogether, because I had a second weakness, which was bursting readily into tears.

But all things pass. I decided, as I was so English, to go to university down south, in Oxford. Once I got there and met the sons of London barristers and the daughters of cabinet ministers, I realized I was not English and posh at all, but Scottish, and squarely middle-class. As I trained as a teacher in Oxford, then worked in London, I even began to feel I wanted to go back permanently to Edinburgh: where I had friends; where I was writing, already, occasional pieces for the *Scotsman*; which was, after all, my native city. I wanted to live there, not in London, and to teach in the schools in Broughton and Leith I had been frightened of as a girl. They looked to me then – they were, they are – strong, splendid comprehensives, better funded than the schools of the south.

Scottish educational institutions were stronger too. Then, as now, Scottish teachers were more firmly regulated than their English counterparts; they could not apply for jobs at schools independently but were recruited and allocated by the local authority, and they had to be registered by the General Teaching Council for Scotland. The GTC ensured, for example, that teachers of French had spent time in France; that everyone had O Level Maths; that all teachers had degrees. I thought this was a good thing, especially as I was smugly sure I had all the right qualifications and experience. I filled in all the forms, and though nine months later I had only been provisionally registered, I resigned my English job and moved north. My provisional registration would let me work in short-term cover jobs, and thus I arrived in Blastmuir, and met Callum and his classmates.

Two years after my original application to the GTC, though, my application was still open. Supply teaching is always rough and I was getting tired of it; I have a memory of removing a child from my class by the headphones of her Walkman. By now it was spring, new job season in schools, but without registration I could not apply for any permanent ones. On the supply circuit, I met another English-qualified teacher who had been waiting three years for permanent registration, then another, then one who had been waiting for five. I met a Canadian who had been waiting for nine. In fact, I couldn't find any teacher qualified outside Scotland who was permanently registered with the GTC. Why wasn't it happening for us? It couldn't be because we were under-qualified, for Canadian teachers are probably the world's most thoroughly trained; and it wasn't because we were unable to teach Scottish exams, for we were teaching them already, in our temporary positions. It felt as if it was because we weren't Scottish, or in my case, not Scottish enough. All of us had written many letters about our applications, but to little effect. No rule was being broken: if you looked at the GTC small print I could see that there was no mandatory time scale for the registration of outsiders; it was always 'discretionary'. In schools, no one seemed to think there was anything wrong with this practice: 'It's natural folk will want the local person,' said one head teacher, and another: 'You can't expect to go ahead of someone who's stayed in Scotland,' while a head of department opined that I might do better with Official X because: 'He kicks with the left foot and you've a Catholic name.' The year was 1991.

Perhaps I should have taken her advice. Instead, being young and easily outraged, I wrote a piece about the whole thing for the *Scotsman*, quoting my Canadian friend's story as well as my own. The results were surprising. Within a week, the *Scotsman* published an article from the GTC saying that English teachers could easily register in Scotland, and a suddenly unfriendly editor refused both the letter and article I offered in reply. Then, and I swear I am not making this up, a senior official of the GTC rang me up at home in the middle of the afternoon and said, not only that I would never be registered, but that I would never again work in any state school in Scotland. He did not leave his name; perhaps he was merely a stray bigot in the GTC building with a free afternoon. But he had access to my file and my phone number and I certainly believed it was true.

I didn't know what to do. I had a fantasy of self-educating in law and taking the GTC to the courts of the European Union. But that would have taken years, and most probably would not have worked anyway; Scotland qualifies as a region when it comes to specialisms like the GTC, and so is not subject to the laws that apply to nations. I interviewed for a private school, but halfway through, after the Head of Department had shown me classrooms that reminded me of the ones I had been a pupil in and told me they studied Muriel Spark only with the lower sets, I burst into tears and ran away.

At the very last minute, I saw the job in Essex. I was interviewed in a prefab hut, so new was the college. They asked me how I would teach *Antony and Cleopatra*, and I told them. Nobody asked me anything about where I came from, or where I'd lived, only what I had learned and what I could do. It was bliss. So I went back to live in London and worked alongside Jamaican and Zoroastrian and Irish teachers in a thriving, dynamic, growing college. No one thought about my national identity, and I tried not to, either. The question which had carried so much weight in my childhood – are you really Scottish? – seemed settled: I wasn't. I married an English man, I had English children, I was fine with it, I always said.

And I am fine. I am better than fine, as Aadil and Shakila constantly remind me. Nevertheless, I miss my country in underground ways, like a covered river running through a town. The Scottish voice, the Scottish hills, my sea, my islands, my precipitous city: they spout up without warning in my dreams and in my fiction and poetry. The independence debate of the last decade fascinates me and alienates me, for I can imagine a Scottish government only as a giant GTC: bureaucratic, anti-English, rejecting anyone with outside experience, asking what foot I kick with. Still, all these years later, thinking about my papers can make me cry. But I suppose the experience gave me some solidarity with Aadil and Shakila, and perhaps some small insight into what institutional racism might feel like. It must be a little similar to the dumbfounding mixture of disgrace and rage I felt when I was told that it was 'natural' that folk would prefer the local person; that I couldn't expect to go ahead of someone who belonged in Scotland, when I looked around and felt that everyone agreed. And now at least when my students tangle with the awful bureaucracy of visa applications, I have had a small experience of having the wrong 'papers' and of being judged by where I had been, rather than what I could do, or, as Dr King once put it, by the 'content of my character'.

About Writing, Secrets, and Being Foreign

Priti, Farah, Priya, and Amina

Priti's Canoe

I was unlocking my bike outside the Inclusion Unit when a small round girl in a hijab approached me. 'Miss,' she said, 'are you the writer?'

I said I was, and solemnly and carefully she handed me an A4 notebook. 'Me and my cousin,' she said, 'wrote a book. Miss B said you would read it.'

Thanks, Miss B. The book was quite hard work. Not only was it in Year 8 handwriting (two different sorts, multiple colours; they'd clearly been taking turns), and long, but it really wasn't my sort of book. It was a version of a teen novel and took place in a summer camp in America. There were mean girls in short skirts and nice girls in white shirts 'teamed' with jeans and a hero with blond hair falling thickly on his polo shirt and a boating accident . . .

'But what I really want to know,' I said, to the small round Priti and her taller, silent cousin Priya, whom Miss B had solemnly gathered for an 'editorial conference', 'what

I really want to know is, why is everyone white? In your book?'

Two pairs of brown eyes gazed at me, baffled, sorrowful.

'Did we get it wrong?' asked Priya.

'Well,' I said, 'not wrong exactly. But you can sort of tell, as a reader, that you haven't been to that American landscape? That camp?'

Priti and Priya cast down their eyes.

'The thing is,' I said, 'canoes don't have engines? Usually.' The girls shuffled their feet, soft and submissive as a box of kittens. I ploughed on.

'I mean,' I said, 'you're both Bengali, right?' They looked up and nodded enthusiastically. 'Well,' I said, 'why not write a story about that?'

'Miss,' said Priya, looking directly at me. 'We are not in books.'

That was news to me. That is, I knew, vaguely, that there were not enough teenage or children's novels, or novels full stop, with people of colour as their protagonists, but I wasn't overly concerned about it. I thought, if anything, that it was a problem that would sort itself out in time, that one shouldn't be too 'politically correct' about these things. I hadn't understood at all how this could affect the way you imagined yourself, your inner life, even your fantasies; above all, your writing.

But in my own early reading there had been white bookish girls everywhere, from *A Little Princess* to *I Capture the Castle* to *Jane Eyre*; girls, moreover, who were the authors of their own books. I remembered how much it bothered me then that Jane Eyre dislikes tall women so palpably, because I was tall; how much easier I found it to love Maggie Tulliver just because she was big and dark; how very much merely hair and skin colour, not to speak of the rest of it – language, nationality, class – just matter in books, perhaps especially to girls. What if, I thought, what if all my childhood reading, all my beloved novels and stories, had not featured a single person who looked like me or spoke to me? How would I feel if I was not in books?

I looked at Priti and Priya, so soft-eyed and polite. They had no advantages at all, no one at home who wrote or read English novels. Nevertheless, they had written a substantial amount of one. It was quite a thing.

'Maybe you should write a novel with Bengali girls in it,' I said. 'There's clearly a need.'

Farah's Secret

She loved me for the dangers I had passed,
And I loved her that she did pity them
OTHELLO, OF DESDEMONA

When you come to a new place, you tell your tale: the story of where you came from and how you got here, because that is the story of who you are. Everyone does this, even if their journeys were short and internal. For migrants, whose dislocations are wide, vivid, and sometimes violent, this telling can become hugely important. Aadil, for example, is very strongly motivated to write, and to write the story of leaving his country: that's how and why I got to know him. Over several years, I watch him tackle the tale over and over again, in verse, in prose, as a play, often very successfully. And then I witness him destroy his efforts, either by physically tearing them up, or with the more developed pieces, with last-minute sabotage: not turning up when he is scheduled to read, withdrawing pieces from competitions, editing contributions to magazines down to the title, replacing subtle protest poems with rhymes copied from the internet, cancelling the play.

Getting him to explain his reasons is always hard, but when we get to it, it's always the same: fear of discovery. Fear that the perfectly understandable, the really very small untruth his parents told when they arrived in this country – that they were of entirely Somali, not mixed, heritage – will be discovered through him; if not through his handsome Kenyan features, then through his words. This lie was terrifying for him as a child, and he is unable to overcome the fear of it in adulthood, even after he and his family get their passports. The lie is a lump in his throat; he has to keep clearing it, he can never start his speech. The lie sends him to study Pharmacy, not English, at university. The lie may be why you haven't heard of him, now, as a writer.

Lies are especially heavy for children – think of the novels *Atonement* or *The Go-Between* – but they hurt adults too. It was easy enough, for example, to persuade Farah, from Iraq, to write about her homeland; words and images came flooding out. But when, after a school poetry reading, I'm approached by her dad, asking in broken English how he can write down his story, things get more complicated. I'm barely home before I get an email from little Farah:

> *good evening, sorry Miss because it's too late for sent the message in this time, but just I'm remind you about my dad story did you remember that? Basically my dad he wants to write all his story from Iraq to Turkey and England. But don't tell anybody about the story, because my dad he does not want*

I reply to Farah carefully, with my standard advice.

> *It was nice to meet your dad. Please tell him that writing a story down is not the same as publishing it in a book. Sometimes it is a good idea to write your story down just for yourself, in your own language. When you have the story safe, then you can move on and decide what you want to do with it. But if you rush along, and worry about how it could be published, or what people might think about it, sometimes that stops you writing it. Maybe we could help with a translator? There might be a student at the university who could help.*

Twenty minutes later, I get the following reply:

> *this message sent to you in wrong, sorry about that means this message not for you for someone else. sorry!!!! don't worry about it. thank you.*
> *Farah*

And minutes later, another.

> *just i'm remind you about my dad story, please do not tell anyone about the story, and also don't tell the university!!!!! that mean don't tell anyone about it please!!! my dad he does not want anybody to know about the story from his friend or anyone please.*

And of course, I say OK, but I don't see Farah again; she drops out of Poetry Group. There is clearly a panic in her house, a panic about stories.

Priya's Poem

After that first meeting, Priti and Priya started coming fairly regularly to my writing groups, and I slowly learned how to teach them. I discovered over those years that poems and stories that directly addressed the migrant experience always got a powerful response. I also discovered that simply telling kids that it was OK to write in their own language, or specifying that their home landscape would be good, and yes to please include it, could have a powerful effect. Over time, Priti had several very creditable goes at the teen novel for Bengalis; she had a splendid sense of melodrama and a good line in kidnappings.

Priya, though, had something else. One day, I went into Miss H's Year 11 second set, a wild set of kids, all beards and facial piercings, and spotted Priya in her floor-length skirt, nearly grown now, but still quiet as a shadow amongst them. I was working on Carol Ann Duffy with the class, getting them to play with the line breaks on the computer screen, interrogating the choices. We were all having so much noisy fun that it wasn't till near the end of the lesson that I saw what Priya was typing.

Homesick

There is that strange smell again, the tang of
cars on the road screeching, not like
the laborious rickshaw in Bangladesh. There is no
inviting market, no smell of spices and sliced fruit –
Look ahead, jump, skip and hop. Hide the fact
you are alienated. Chew on the candy floss.
It melts in your mouth. Such foreign stuff!

It sounded like Duffy, but it also sounded like Priya – a super-charged, sonorous, sophisticated Priya. She had never written like that before – the irony, the confidence, the assonance, the eccentric, powerful diction; but she had also never before addressed her migrant experience directly. Perhaps the two were related?

'Miss,' said Priya, disturbed by my slack-jawed staring. 'Is it OK? I wrote my own.'

Amina's Birthday

Amina used to be one of my writing students. She was so bright; I thought she had gone to university. Now, though, she has turned back up at school, a support worker for asylum seekers. I ask her what she thinks the problem with Farah's family might be. Don't they have their papers? I'd understood they were that very rare thing: government-sponsored refugees.

'Yes,' says Amina, 'but that doesn't mean they aren't hiding something. All refugees are hiding something. Have you ever met one that wasn't?'

I haven't, but my experience isn't as wide as hers. I say: 'I think it's because they only get one chance. They arrive at the airport or whatever, and then they have to tell exactly the right story to get in. It's really hard.'

Amina is nodding at me vigorously. 'And then they have to stick to it forever! And they make mistakes, and they don't speak English. It's impossible. And people smugglers, they tell them to lie.'

'Do you think everyone uses people smugglers?' I ask.

Amina's pretty features are flushing; her voice is rising. 'Yes! How else do you get out? How do you get across the Mediterranean? All the people who actually get here, they started with money! They had houses, cars, family, and they sold it all to get here! They gave it all to people smugglers. And when you get here, they tell you to lie! That's what they do. They take your money, and tell you to lie, because then they have a hold on you.'

And of course it had happened to her. Amina came here when she was three from the Indian subcontinent. Her father has a claim to British citizenship through his mother, which should have worked out fine. But her parents, in ignorance and fear, had put themselves in the hands of people smugglers, brutal ones, who kept her father at sweated labour for years. At one point, her mother went to prison.

'Why do you think I'm not at university?' asks Amina. 'Do you think, if I had clean papers, I wouldn't be there in a second?' And of course, she would. She's hugely clever, and desperate to learn.

The family's affairs are now being painfully unpicked by a better lawyer, paid for, in part, by Amina. But there is a lot to do.

'They made me lie about my birthday!'

'Your birthday? Why? To make you younger?'

'I was only three! No, so there would be something wrong on every passport. Something to feel bad about. So now I've got two birthdays, the real one and the passport one. Pakistani and English. But you know what? So have a lot of Pakistanis.'

She shows me on her phone an invitation to a party for another of my former students, smiling in a glittering headscarf. 'For her real birthday!' she says. 'Pakistanis only.'

'I thought Saira went to university?' I said. She certainly ought to have.

'No! She's in the same boat as me. Hasn't got her papers, so she can't go. She pretends it's because she doesn't want to, but she does!'

Amina wants to do more than go to university; she wants to write. She's good; I'm always encouraging her. I tell her to write down Saira's story, or maybe Farah's. Later that evening, she texts me:

I'm trying to write but it's hard. The lying, the whole family lying, it stops you writing. It's the shame. This shame that we shouldn't have to carry.

Priya's Poems

So by the time Priya hit the sixth form, I knew she was talented, and I knew she was writing. I set her off on projects, gave her particular things to read. All the same, when I first pulled her poem out of my pigeon hole and read it and felt my eyes prickle and the hairs on the back of my neck rise, I also thought she could not have written it, no sixth-former could. This poem, I mean.

My Mother Country
I don't remember her
in the summer,
lagoon water sizzling,
the kingfisher leaping,
or even the sweet honey mangoes
they tell me I used to love.
I don't remember
her comforting garment,
or her saps of date trees,
providing the meagre earnings
for those farmers
out there
in the gulf
under the calidity of the sun,

or the mosquitoes
droning in the monsoon,
or the tipa tapa of the rain,
on the tin roofs,
dripping on the window,
I think.

Because, after all, Priya wasn't academically brilliant. She did come to Poetry Group, but not always, only at lunchtimes, when she could fit it in. Her A Levels were in Economics, Ethics, and Politics, and she was usually to be found in the library, with a dry textbook, working like stink. She read a lot in Bengali though. Could the poem be a translation? I googled it, typing in first the title, then the whole piece, but nothing came up.

In the process, I read the poem again. As a speech act, there was something very familiar about it. That trick of opening like a Japanese fan, of furling out from a neat dark cover to display the gorgeous, sensual landscape of Bangladesh, then folding itself back into a pose of meek denial – how many times had I heard that from our students? 'I came from Somalia/Afghanistan/Brazil when I was six/nine/three, Miss, but I don't remember. I don't remember anything about it.' And what was it Priya told me the other week? About the importance of the word 'mother' in Bengali: *We say mother country, Miss, mother fruit . . . ?*

Calidity, indeed. Well, Priya was devoted to her thesaurus – 'calidity' would be exactly the sort of obscure word she would jackdaw away, for the glitter of it. And she loved patternings and echoes; 'meagre earnings', halfway to a palindrome, was exactly the sort of phrase she doodled in her margins. And the rich sound, those lamenting 'o's, droning in the monsoon, and the irony? Well, I'd heard them before, in the response to Duffy.

So I decided 'My Mother Country' really was Priya's work. I sent Priya an email – *flipping amazing, what have you been reading?* – then typed up a fresh copy of the poem in Times New Roman, removing a stray comma, marvelling again at the shape. I printed out a copy and taped it to the staffroom tea urn (someone read it out at a Senior Leadership Team meeting later in the day), then made another, and took it across to Miss H. She stuck it on her door, just above the handle, so that everyone entering or leaving her classroom had to read it. Then I copied off a class set and took it into my next scheduled lesson, Miss T's Year 7s, and read it to them, and asked them for a poem beginning: *I don't remember.*

Afterwards, I leafed through the results in the staffroom, dazzled. Priya's poem was a magic key; it had unlocked, in half an hour, thirty poems. Sana had written about her mother tongue: *How shameful, shameful, forgotten.* Ismail, who had never written a poem before, who rarely spoke, covered three pages with sensual remembrance, ending: *I don't remember the fearless boy I used to be / no, I don't remember my country, Bangladesh.* So many of them, and so good, so fresh, and, like Priya's poem, with such sophisticated soundscapes – it was freakish, especially when you considered that almost all of the kids in Miss T's class had two languages. Most of them, in fact, had lost a country and a language before they were ten.

And that was when I first thought: maybe that loss isn't something I have to compensate for. Maybe that loss is a poet's gain. The kids in that class didn't have foreign accents; they had picked up English exactly as it was spoken around them, as only kids can. So they must have been able to listen to the sounds of language, as well as the sense, with extra, children-only, other-language-only ears. Extra sound awareness: that must make poets. Also that shock of dislocation that had turned them in on themselves; which made them listen to their inner voice; the period each had gone through *when silence itself was my friend*, as Priya had put it, in another poem: doesn't that also make a writer, that sort of orphaning? So many of the children in our school had a loss to mourn, a country, a family – and in the end, isn't that what poetry is for? *By the rivers of Babylon, we sat down and wept.* A spell to bring things back.

If all that was the case, then our school wasn't a 'disadvantaged comprehensive' when it came to poetry. In fact, it stood at an advantage, rather as the Western Rift Valley stands to long-distance runners. Our students were like those Kenyan children who ran ten miles barefoot to school and grew up to dominate the world in long-distance running; hardened by the low oxygen and harsh peaks, exposed to great beauty and great fear, fitted out, just by their daily lives, for the very longest distances. In which case, I thought, in which case it is about time I did a Rift Valley on the kids, and trained up a team, and we won something. Specifically, it is time someone, let's say Priya, won the Foyle Young Poets of the Year Award.

I'd judged this annual competition, which is run by the national Poetry Society, back in 2006, and then taught the residential writing course – an Arvon course – that is the prize for the young winners. It may not sound like much of a prize, a week in the country with fourteen others and a couple of poets, but the famous annual Foyle course has evolved into a powerful intervention. By the time I read Priya's poem, the Foyle group I'd taught a few years earlier were scything through Oxbridge, publishing pamphlets with our most prestigious publishing houses, writing for the national press, and all the time networking frantically with each other like an artsy version of the Bullingdon Club. By mixing a group of exceptionally talented youngsters together, many of them privileged but a couple definitely not, that course had, almost violently, changed most of their lives. I wanted some of that for my students: not just the poetry, but the sense of entitlement, and yes, the networking too. The thing called cultural capital. Imagine the netful just one kid could bring back, I thought. Imagine the sweet, soulful kids I had taught on the Foyle course being confronted with Priya's experience.

I remembered that the rower Steve Redgrave was discovered by his shoes. An enterprising teacher had decided that his comprehensive lads should get in a rowing eight, so he organized the boat, then went into the boys' changing room to see who had the biggest feet. I decided to start my quest for prizes in a similar way; by looking for poets' footprints, targeting students like Priya, with the same special abilities she had. I wanted students tempered by loss; turned inward instead of outward; who were quiet;

who read; the ones who still seemed to live in two worlds and two languages; who still seemed unassimilated, other: *foreign*. I thought I'd start with just girls, because I could think of several new arrivals who would be happier that way. And so it was that I asked my English colleagues to recommend some Very Quiet Foreign Girls, and because they are not only brilliant, but always get my jokes, they immediately understood, and obliged.

Miss H said, 'Oh yes, I have one for you. Kala only came last term, but she wrote something that was quite definitely a poem.' Miss W introduced me to Shakila. Miss T, who is prone to melodrama, said, 'Fatima! *So I left it there, my teddy bear, its blank eyes staring* – these lines are forever graven on my heart.' And Miss P said: 'You can use my room.' Which was particularly generous, as Miss P is very tidy, and I am not. Miss A raised an eyebrow dryly and suggested: 'Possibly find another name? You'll have a problem getting all that on a T-shirt.'

Miss A is always right. The group, officially the 'Other Countries Poetry Group', was held every Thursday lunchtime for two terms in Miss P's tidy room. It was quiet there, and, when the bell rang for tutor time, and the clamour of teenagers rushing to class rose round us like water, we had a special dispensation to stay on in our sealed chamber, our airlock, writing. As well as Priya, Priti, and Shakila, there was Priya's younger sister Disha, and their anxious friend Neelam, all from Bangladesh; then Fatima of the melancholy teddy bear, and Saira, with the thick glasses and infinite naiveté, both from India; Kala, Miss H's silent, traumatized arrival from Sri Lanka; and, white-blonde among all the black plaits and hijabs, and younger than the others, Eszter, from Hungary.

We did my usual thing: we read a poem, then wrote one. But they wrote brilliantly; the thing I was looking for, that special, foreign ability to hear poetic sounds and sense shape, surfaced in spades. So Kala, who rarely spoke, who scarcely had, you would say to talk to her, any English, who cannot possibly have understood half the words of Carol Ann Duffy's 'Originally', nevertheless responded to it in a way that showed she had heard the rhymes, and how they chimed with the sense, and, more widely, how much she heard the 'l's in English, the bells:

> I remember a room, next to my class
> One that was always empty, until
> We heard the bell. Then
> It was filled with our voices, filled
> With the jokes we used to tell.
> Then I left it
> To be here.
> Where all rooms fill
> With people I don't know.

Shakila, meanwhile, seemed to have the floor plan of a poem in her head and to need help only with filling in the blocks. She would call out to me for words, urgently, her black, almond-shaped eyes snapping, slim fingers blossoming: *Thingies!*

'Miss! A thingy! A bird. You are in the desert. It is not an owl!'

'Vulture?'

'Yes! Spell please!' And her high-set, starched hijab – did she have extra ears under there? – would rustle earnestly as she wrote it down.

We know that people learn foreign languages best by immersion – so why not poetry? My quiet foreign girls seemed to learn form as they learned English: rapidly, and not word by word or brick by brick, but wholesale, structure by structure, arch by arch. They were not put off by difficulty – the stronger and stranger a poem, in fact, the more rhetorical and 'poem-y', the more they liked it. So when we read Auden, for instance – 'On this Island' – the girls reproduced the awed and awesome tone of that most peculiar poem, and its clotted sound, without seeming to think about it, and effortlessly translated its English cliff into their own landscapes. Eszter wrote about a Hungarian plain where the light was 'riding its cloud horse', and enjoined us to 'remember it / the free and wild wind / like a gentle touch'. Shakila picked up on the verb form, and, after shouting for many 'thingies', created a poem about arrival at the airport, clutching 'bags full of dictionaries', all in the imperative:

> See the country
> like a journey
> unfold right there.
> Let your life change.

And Priya, who was by now, it seemed fair to say, motoring, conjured up a magical Sylheti junglescape, where a Bengal tiger 'obsolete as an emperor / breathes'.

By May, Miss P's room was filled with babble. Sometimes it was frustrated: Shakila on her furious quest for words; the low moans of Neelam suddenly giving up mid-poem, and insisting that each line she had written, each word, was in some indescribable way wrong. Mostly, though, it was cheerful. Tiny Fatima of the sad bear proved not to be melancholy at all, but impish – given to delivering runaway rants on the merits of *Twilight*. She wrote a long poem in an invented language – half English, half Urdu – and giggled at it until she fell off the seat and kicked up, under her long robe, outlandish high heels.

Disha and Neelam formed an alliance of satire, writing deliberate, dark counterpoints to Priya's exquisite sun-filled laments. Both of them had had the experience of leaving Bangladesh as young children, and then returning as teenagers, only to be as alienated and terrified by their country's poverty as they felt welcomed by its warmth. They could not say enough dark things about it, and at the same time, they could not love it enough, or leave the subject alone. One day, Disha wrote an utterly triumphant poem, a piece about Bangladesh that ran through a series of grand metaphors in grand language, discarding them all, and ended: "And so, my poem is my country / my home country / and my country is poor." And she read it out, and looked over to her gifted, lyrical sister, and gave a tiny nod.

We didn't win.

We sent all the Foreign Girl poems into the Foyle competition, including 'My Mother Country', the obsolete tiger, and the cloud-horse, but got not so much as a mention. I was merely sad about this – it's a huge competition – until the winning poems were published alongside portraits and bios of the lucky poets. Then, I found myself studying them obsessively. They were all white! How could this have happened? And a large number of them seemed to go to boarding school. (Not that their schools were published; I discovered this by noting the winners' home counties, and then typing in their names next to the name of their nearest prestigious private school on Google – as in, Camilla Poshperson, Cranborne Chase – and up they popped, one after the other, on the hockey or debate team.) I was shocked.

Because my assumption, when I sent out the Foreign Girl poems, was that they would be especially welcome because of their foreignness. When I'd judged the competition myself, I'd been on the lookout for the migrant experience, and there hadn't been much in evidence. I thought that was because not enough migrant kids knew about the competition, and that my poets would be, if anything, at an advantage in such a field. In short, I thought there might be some of that much-vaunted thing, political correctness, around to help my students out. Clearly, though, not.

What had happened? I studied and studied the winning poems. They were good, of course they were good, but they were not longer or more complex or more literary than Priya's poem. What they did share, and what I saw suddenly for the first time with a shock, as if coming back to my home city by water after a lifetime of approaching it by road, was a white landscape, one with lakes and low hills and houses filled with grandmothers in aprons who baked sponge cakes; houses with deckchairs, and copies of *National Geographic*, all foggy with restrained regret. This was the landscape that was recognized as poetic; Priya's bright and humid Bangladesh was not.

In the end, I was so cross I wrote a letter, which was listened to courteously, and in subsequent years, things have changed radically; though it remains true that my only young poets of colour who have won any poetry competition have been selected by judges of colour. I repeated the process many times; I sent out 'My Mother Country' and the others to five more poetry competitions for young people, and, when more poems set in that white landscape were preferred, sent more rude letters. The one to the fifth competition was very rude; I got into a row. Was I accusing them of prejudice? Well, yes, I suppose I was. And I still suppose they were; that most people are prejudiced; that I am, that prejudice happens in the reading of poetry as well as everything else. I also think that if you acknowledge it, and try and set aside, you can see more: that is a gift that Priya's poem has given me.

Another gift is that I now read more widely. The other day, while trekking across the vast landscape that is Tagore, the national poet of Bangladesh, Priya's favourite reading matter, I finally came upon what is probably the source poem for 'My Mother Country': 'I Cannot Remember My Mother', the simple lament that Tagore wrote when he was fifty for the mother he lost when he was three.

I cannot remember my mother
but when in the early autumn morning

the smell of the shiuli flowers floats in the air
the scent of the morning service in the temple
comes to me as the scent of my mother.

And the poem quenched my anger, as great poems will.
Perhaps, I thought, the problem is simply that 'My Mother
Country' sounds as if it were written by a fifty-year-old,
and so doesn't fit with the teenage poems in competitions.
Perhaps the judges could not believe, as I didn't believe
at first, that seventeen-year-olds can write like that, or
go through loss like that, or be as old as that in their
minds, and so they put the poem aside. And if it is also
the case that we have not tuned in to this voice yet, the
voice of our new England, an English inflected with all
the accents of the world, with the mass migration of the
early years of the twenty-first century, the voices of the
Very Quiet Foreign Girls, then perhaps I can understand
why, and think how lucky I am to work in a place where
I can hear it.

Priya herself has no regrets. She values her writing,
and her journey, for itself. And in school we continue to
value this poem especially. It has created, in poetry workshops, a thousand daughter poems. We have published it
in anthologies, put it on the website, and blown it up to
six foot high, framed it, and hung it in the English corridor:
a permanent, life-size reminder of the Very Quiet Foreign
Girls. When we showed the result to Priya she gazed at it
for a long while, pleased, then said: 'Look, all the "o"s.' The
poem is indeed studded with them: *honey, love, mangoes,*
don't, don't, mosquitoes, monsoon. Blown up to the size of

my hand, the 'o's look like portholes, or lifebelts, or pools, and now each year new generations of students gaze through them, or hang on to them, or dive into them, and start to write about what they can't remember.

About the Hijab

Imani's Argument

Perhaps half the girls I teach wear hijab to school; black stretchy cotton ones for the younger girls, elaborately pinned shawls for the sixth-formers. A hijab now, to me, signals a probably good student, a potentially excellent one. Shakila, Disha, Priya, and Imani were all hijabis and also some of my most talented poets. I knew them extremely well; I met their parents, I took them on residential trips, and I never saw their (Asian/silky/curly?) hair in eight years.

All four of these women, and I think all the hijabi girls I teach, cover up more than their mothers. Muslim women in the Indian subcontinent universally wore a loose, light scarf in the last years of the twentieth century and very often still do. Women in North African countries wore a head wrap. The burqa and the niqab came only from Arabia, and they came before Islam, from desert countries where it was practical to wear long, loose, enveloping garments and to cover the face; it is only in the last few decades that these garments have spread. In our city now, many young Pakistani women wear the niqab, and almost all Muslim women wear a scarf that pins tightly under the jawline and covers the whole plait behind.

Imani has a fierce argument as to why this should be so. (In fact many of the girls do, but Imani – tiny, Tanzanian, and terrifyingly articulate – puts it best, and has even made prize-winning speeches about it.) Imani says: Look around you. Look at Instagram or just down the street. Look at the young girls in their tight dresses, and mini-skirts, their breasts out on show like buns! (I think she might mean Susie.) Look at them trying to run in their high heels! (She definitely means Kristell.) And then look at the modest young girl on the other side of the street, airy in her long dress, modest in her veil, comfortable in her soft, hidden shoes. Who is wearing the imprisoning garment? Who is the freer in her mind?

And, of course, she is right. If I could put a burqa on Susie and Kristell tomorrow, I would. A year or two of being invisible to the male gaze, of going home quietly to study, could only be liberating, and enabling too, of the rest of their lives. But I am suspicious of some of the rest of Imani's argument. Imani is very sporty herself, and her long dress visibly restricts her. Not every gaze is sexualizing, and not all sexualizing is desperately offensive; because looking is a healthy thing that people do, and so is desiring, and women do both. There is a disturbing undercurrent of good girl/bad girl in Imani's argument, and it's important to say that nothing that Susie or Kristell ever wear, however brief, entitles them to any abuse, ever.

I would also like to observe that it is possible to wear

a flirty hijab, like Samira's leopard-patterned one. And that Farida's dress may be loose and floor-length, but it still manages to show the beautiful lines of her figure when she hitches it tight around her as she sits by the basketball courts; and when she tucks her hijab that bit neater round her ear with one tiny, manicured, be-ringed hand, it drives Izzat visibly bonkers. Even Imani started wearing head wraps instead of shawls in university. She looked brilliant, because she has such a strong skull shape and elegant neck, and also more African, which she is, and it was not immodest in any way.

Also: Amina comes from a strict Pakistani background and remains a devout Muslim. She has thought carefully about the whole issue and doesn't wear the hijab. She has her hair cut to her jaw, and wears modest clothes as the Koran says, but they are pretty and no sort of uniform. She is tiny and beautiful, but this is not what you notice about her; you see her intelligence and her warmth. Amina walks effortlessly down the street, hampered by neither heels nor long skirts, and if men whistle, it hurts her, much more than it would hurt Susie, but she ignores them. She makes a straw man of Imani's argument, because she is so supple, and decided, and so very much herself.

About Uniform

Elsa, Connor, and Saira

I'm in favour of uniform, and here are the children why.

Because of Elsa

Elsa is small and freckled and mostly silent. You could not say she was talented, exactly, but she is keen; she comes to Poetry Group very regularly, and writes small, sad poems, nearly square. She is particularly keen on having her work typed out; when she was absent once she brought me an extra square sad poem on a sheet of A4 for me to tackle. Miss B is very taken by this progress, and when we are offered a trip to London we agree: a place for Elsa. But we can't get her mum to sign the form.

Forms are an endless nuisance; we expect delay. We anticipate it, in fact; we photocopy extra forms, we dole them out several times, we nag, we write notes in planners, we phone home. Two days before the trip, this has worked for everyone but Elsa, and Miss B is making arrangements for her to stay in school, when, on my way home at nearly six at night, I spot Elsa walking away from the Co-op, holding a loaf of bread. I catch her up, and she is so alarmed, she walks faster, pulling her hood up over her heavy wings of dark greasy hair.

'Don't you want to come on the trip?' I ask her.

'Yeah,' she says, surprised, outraged.

'What about the form then?'

'I got it,' she says.

'Well then, could we have it?'

'I lost it,' she says, with equal conviction. We have stopped at the gated entrance to the flats behind the Co-op, where Elsa seems to live, and I have one of my brilliant ideas. I have a spare photocopied form right here in my bag. Why doesn't Elsa just pop upstairs and get her mum to sign it?

'You want to see my mum?' says Elsa. And I say no, it isn't necessary, I can wait right there.

There is a long pause. Elsa looks at her small, turned-in feet. 'But,' I say, 'I could come in. If that would help. If it would help if I explained.'

And so I fall down an Alice in Wonderland rabbit hole and find myself in another land, in a small red room with a loud television and an acrid, woody smell, where a woman in a velour dressing gown is huddled in an armchair, and a yellow bird bashes my face like a slap.

'They like to fly about,' says the woman. And I see that there is a bird cage in front of her with an open door, and two canaries loose in the room, and seed and bird droppings everywhere underfoot. Elsa still has her coat on. She stands quietly by the door, feet pressed together.

'I'm Elsa's teacher,' I say nervously. 'I just bumped into her and I thought . . . There's this trip to London. I expect she told you?'

'Ain't heard nothing about it,' says the woman. 'We can't pay this month.'

'It's free,' I say. 'I wondered – could you just sign this form?' And I hand her the form, and she takes it and studies it.

'Uumph,' she says. 'Dunno.'

Suddenly, Elsa appears with a pen. 'Mum,' she says, 'just there, sign there.' And the woman puts down a scribble, and I realize she can't read.

'Miss has to go,' says Elsa, and I can't wait.

Afterwards I tell the story to Miss B, who nods.

'You wouldn't know,' I say. 'Elsa looks quite normal in school.'

'No,' says Miss B. 'Lost property is a wonderful thing.'

And it turns out to be Miss B who greets Elsa every morning for breakfast club, and unlocks the shower in PE for her, and hands out clean uniform. It is Miss B who whizzes the clothes round the school washing machine, the one bought for PE kit, every week.

Miss B says Elsa only ever misses one day of school each year, and that is Red Nose Day, when no uniform is worn.

Because of Connor

Connor is never quite late, but always last-minute. He is also never quite without uniform, but always has something misplaced; he is wearing his sports trainers already, he has a baseball cap on, a jacket slung over his shoulder. So every morning, Miss P tells him off, makes him remove the offending garment, and sends him on his way with a flea in his ear. Miss P is our most imposing, old-fashioned, scary member of staff. 'He never gets any better,' she says, 'so we have to conclude that he likes a telling-off.'

And probably he does. Miss P is scary, but she is also very fair, and very clear. Connor is small, undergrown, unable to progress. He has the small head and mask-like face that are the markers of foetal alcohol syndrome. He comes from a cruel, chaotic home where most attention comes as abuse. He has chosen this engagement with Miss P. Each morning, she and the uniform tell Connor that he is in a boundaried place now, where people care what he wears, and care if he keeps the rules.

Uniform is a very safe thing to kick against, just as Miss P is a safe person to kick.

Because of the Poor Table

Once, wearing my poet hat, I visit the poshest and most over-subscribed state primary in the city, and one of the few not to have a uniform. Year 5 look comfy and cheery in their non-uniform outfits, but when the teacher tells me that the less able children are gathered at one table and she will support me there, I am shocked to find that she does not need to tell me which table that is. It's the one with the boy in the Manchester United shirt, the girl in the tracksuit, and her friend with the pierced ears, tiara, and leggings. The table with no one at all sporting outfits from the Boden catalogue, or shoes from Clarks. This school does very well generally in its SATs, but not by its few disadvantaged kids, who lag dreadfully. I don't expect the Poor Table, and the ease with which it is identified, helps.

Because of Saira

Saira is the youngest of three devoted Pakistani sisters. They are orphans; their father died, and they are being raised by their constantly ill mother and two bullying, much older brothers. Recently, the brothers have taken to going to the strict Wahhabi mosque, and the older sisters, who are in the sixth form, where there is no uniform, are kitted out in floor-length dresses and tight hot hijabs. Saira is still in Year 9, so she can't wear that kit to school, she's not allowed. She wears the widely despised, baggy, Terylene school trousers instead. The older sisters have grown heavy and womanish already and spend lunchtimes in the library. Saira, though, can be seen at lunchtime round the basketball hoops, jumping and running. Saira is very butch-looking altogether, with square shoulders and a distinct moustache. She adds a baseball cap, quite often, in school colours, and when she punts the ball into the hoop she looks utterly happy, joyous, even; healthy and moving and alive in those ugly uniform trousers.

On the Church in Schools

Tess, Jude, and Oldest One

Tyneham is a 'ghost village' in the Purbeck peninsula in
Dorset. It's a 'ghost' because it was requisitioned as an
emergency measure in 1943 for the army to practise
shooting at, in, and through. After the war, though the
government promised otherwise, it was not given back to
its ancestral tenants; instead, the army kept it and the
surrounding, lovely, Lulworth Ranges. Tyneham sank
under gunfire as if drowning in a reservoir, and lost its
roofs, and its Great Hall, and became a picturesque ruin,
golden stones in green hills.

These days, it's open to visitors on weekends and Bank
Holidays. Then, the army ceases its training exercises and
making of loud pops, lowers the red flags over its gateways,
and in come the general public; on foot, in Range Rovers,
and by the coachload. One year, we bring our children, all
under nine, to see this village, 'frozen in time'.

Frozen it certainly is, but the year does not seem to be
1943. With its single narrow street pointing to a church
full of tombs, Tyneham seems stuck at some much earlier

point, some sepia era when all things were bright and beautiful, and the poor man at his gate, doffing his cap. This is Thomas Hardy country – it says so on lots of signs, as if it were a synonym for 'rural and picturesque' – but I can only see the dark, political side of Hardy, here. Here are the dank, dark corridors of the dairy just like the one where Tess worked; here is the servants' path to the Great House, just like the one Tess took to be raped and abused – though if you look up, here is also the humbling beauty Hardy wrote about, the huge, overarching sky.

In the workers' street, it is seven steps across a cottage, yet we read on the wall that two adults and ten children lived there at the last census in the 1930s. We try to work out where the beds could have fitted and can't. We consider the single tap that served all the houses; we hop over the scars of the medieval-style rigs allocated to the villagers by the landlord. When the evacuation happened, the villagers were compensated only for the vegetables they were growing in these rigs. They didn't own any other piece of Tyneham, though they and their forebears had lived and worked on this land all their lives.

I've always been a Hardy-sceptic, in fact, never really credited that rural life in England can have been as primitive or humourless as he described it in the late nineteenth century. But by the time we get to the church, I am revising all that. Here, lilies are laid on the stone that remembers the village boys slaughtered in the First World War, but all the other tombs inside the church are for just one family, the Bonds. They owned this village for centuries, just as in Hardy's novel the D'Urbervilles owned Tess's village.

The Bonds owned the church too, for the rectors were all scions – often younger brothers – of the squires in the Great Hall. Sometimes, the rector and squire were even the same person. In 1880, for instance, when the church was improved and the rectory built, one Nathaniel Bond did both jobs. He lived in the Great Hall, and the rectory was created for his curate, who, to add to the doubling effect, was married to his wife's twin. That, I reckon, could go straight in a Hardy novel: nominative determinism, twins, the lot.

Nathaniel Bond was an improver. He also built the Tyneham village school – or rather, he recycled a tithe barn by the church for the purpose, a building approximately the size of the new rectory drawing room. Now, with its pretty pitched roof restored, the school is such a draw to visitors I can hardly squeeze my children in. I decline an offer of a pinafore for my youngest. I hiss at my children, who are in danger of enjoying themselves, to look at how inadequate the place is. The low, narrow space with platform and iron forms was intended for sixty scholars; there must have been barely room to sit down. There was also barely any learning on offer; just reading, writing, and figuring, administered by one teacher and one assistant. The pupils left at twelve, and the paths from here led only to servitude: the farm, the fishing beach, and the servants' hall. Thomas Hardy, I now see, was not even slightly laying it on a bit thick. I inwardly promise to never again giggle at *Jude the Obscure*, not even the 'Done because we are too menny' line when the children hang themselves to save their parents money. This is serious.

Imagine the school, urge the helpful laminated cards on the benches, *in the days of Nathaniel Bond!* So I do: the children offering prayers of thanks to the provider of their education, who was also their spiritual leader and the man who owned all their property except their cabbages; the man who owned, effectively, their parents. There must have been a young Jude the Obscure in this classroom, a clever Tess Durbeyfield. They must have had questions, and part of the purpose of this school was to give them an Establishment answer. Nathaniel Bond was not generous when he opened this school; he was self-interested. If he hadn't done it, his next generation of servants might have turned to the Sunday Schools of the thriving Methodist Movement; might, in the fine West Country way, have rebelled against this awful alliance of landlord and church.

But no one rebels any more. Even here in the West Country, the Methodists and the Church of England, Chapel Street and Church Street, are more or less united. Here in Tyneham, no one is angry. The question of how Nathaniel Bond would pass into heaven through the Needle's Eye gate when he has such a lot of baggage on his very fat camel is moot. And moot, too – a gentle, cloudy, watercolour moot – the question of how the church of Jesus Christ, who was against property, acquired so much; the question of why this school does not belong to the people who quarried and cut every stone of it, who built it, who maintained it, who used it. It is only me, I feel, who sees this school as a museum of serfdom and daylight robbery. For everyone else, the church and school are lovely ghosts from a gentler age, from the land of lost content.

Which is also how the law of this country treats church schools: as a pretty, harmless, kindly antique. But they are not: they are alive and thriving and have their ideology generously supported by the state. About a third of the schools in England still belong to either the Catholic Church or the Church of England, and most of them operate under the Voluntary Aided system. (There is another, much smaller set of church schools called 'Voluntary Controlled', and these get more Church funding in exchange for more Church character; the two are constantly and chronically confused.) The Voluntary Aided arrangement means that all of the day-to-day running and expenses of the school are handed over to the local council, while the Church retains ownership of the buildings and land. The Church also keeps the right to give assemblies, enforce spiritual visits, have a presence on the governing body, and appoint the head teacher only from among their faithful.

Which is quite a lot of power, especially when you consider that in return, the Church has no statutory obligation at all. There is a widespread myth that the Church gives 10 per cent of funding to church schools, but this has never been the case. The clue is in the name, *Voluntary* Aided. The Catholic Church or C of E supply their VA schools each year, on a strictly *voluntary* basis, with about 10 per cent of the costs of maintaining *the buildings*, nothing else.

And even as we are slamming the car doors to leave Tyneham, I am wondering about the detail of that. Because my kids go to a Voluntary Aided church school. This wasn't my choice; most of the primary schools in my county are

C of E, and this one is yards from my door. It's probably a bit more middle-class than the state one half a mile away, but it still doesn't have a great reputation. Ofsted says it is 'satisfactory', which means it isn't, very. People keep leaving. During Oldest One's first year, ten children left his class as places came up in neighbouring, churchier schools. I always asked the parents why, and they said peculiar, Nathaniel Bond-like things in response: 'St Egg's has lovely windows,' was one, and 'Gillian just wants more discipline; she's crying out for blackboards,' was another. Gillian was five.

The other schools had better SAT results, was the truth. They had more middle-class pupils. And they protected these goods with a method to make Nathaniel Bond proud: they specified church attendance criteria on their admissions policies. Being a *baptized C of E child whose parents are active church members of St Mungo's, St Egg's, or St James's (Attended more than once a month for more than twelve months. Must be supported by evidence from the vicar)* made you a top-priority pupil for the school with the lovely windows, and Gillian's super-anxious mother had duly joined St Egg's, even though she was an atheist. Not that this hypocrisy was particular to our area. I personally knew an Orthodox Jew leading the church lesson in Stoke Newington, and a respectable don's family who had their children baptized twice, in Catholic and Church of England churches, so as to give them a back-up option for primary school.

I have not done any of these things. I am glad our school doesn't have church attendance criteria. I think praying for entrance stinks; stinks of the lilies in the church of Tyneham, of the class system and everything that lies behind it. On the other hand, Oldest One's year group is down to three-quarters full, and the corresponding funding is down too. I'd like the school to be fuller and more prosperous. I'd like Oldest One to have more middle-class classmates. I'd also like him to feel free to go to the toilet during the day. At the moment, he won't, because he thinks the lavatory is too horrible. My friend on the governors' board says that if we agreed to add in some church attendance criteria on our entrance policy, which might make us more popular, and would in time boost church attendance, the church would give us some more money for our buildings, and we could build a new loo.

Let's review that again, I think, as we climb the hill to the Tolpuddle Martyrs Memorial. Today, in 2008, we are being asked to pray for new urinals, just as the children of Tyneham prayed in thankfulness for their landlord allowing them a corner of the land they worked in which to have an inadequate education. How did we get here?

Well, let's go back another twenty years: Easter, 1988. I am sitting on a train platform, giggling my head off with an older teacher, a tall, glamorous Jamaican woman, whom I have just met and like a lot. We are giggling because we have both just run away from a job interview in the nearby school. They'd left us in the staffroom while they interviewed the third candidate, and, with touching unanimity, we had raised eyebrows at each other, then rolled our eyes towards the door, then nipped off.

All the way down the drive we ripped the place to shreds; it was a Voluntary Controlled C of E comprehensive that had somehow fallen into the hands of an evangelical branch of the church. The English store cupboard was full of antiquated, priggish novels. Year 9 had been asked to write haiku on the true meaning of Easter for homework. There were, and this finished us both off, several acrostic poems on *the Crucifixion* on the walls. Neither of us thought twice about abandoning the interview. As my companion said, there were plenty more jobs around because only a nutter like me would go into teaching in 1988, and only a nutter like her would stay.

'Why does anyone go to that school?' I ask her. I couldn't understand it. Parents could choose a school in the local area in 1988, and there was a perfectly normal-looking comprehensive just down the road. My new friend waxes serious.

'Race,' she says, 'didn't you notice? Not a lot of black kids in there. And this is a really mixed area.'

Then, seeing me blanch, she softens her line. 'Parents,' she says. 'They all like to feel they're getting something a bit special. Keep the riff-raff out. Anything will do, really. You take it from me, all parents are crazy.'

'Well,' I say, 'I still think that place can't survive. The state of the desks! They were a hundred years old. I'm definitely going to teach in a comprehensive. A real one, I mean. Nothing Voluntary Aided for me.' And then my train arrives and I cheerfully get aboard.

But it was a faster train than I'd thought, and I had mistaken the direction of travel. As we sat on that platform, the Education Reform Act, which gave parents the right to choose their children's school *regardless of area*, was passing through parliament. By the time I got my first job, it was in place. Almost at once, the school with the crucifixion acrostics was in receipt of far more applications, some from miles away, than the lovely multi-racial comprehensive where I started work. As my school suffered and shrank under the ensuing decade of Tory austerity, Acrostic High grew a thick hedge of church-attending, bell-ringing admissions criteria, impenetrable to all but the most literate and determined. It grew its middle-class population, ruthlessly took parental donations, and thrived. When exam results started to be collated and published, Acrostic's motivated, middle-class pupils made it look marvellous, and it began to build up a reputation as an academic powerhouse. The nearby churches filled up with prospective parents. The bells had never been so well rung. A journalist wrote a feature on the school in 1995 for a national paper and concluded that it did so well because of its 'lovely ethos'.

And then, finally, just in time to save state education, Labour got in. They upped funding all round. They raised teachers' pay. But they did not, as they had promised, stop selection or do anything about the religious divisions between schools. In fact, Blair declared war on the 'bog-standard comprehensive' and encouraged all sorts of specialization. Under Labour, Acrostic High prospered even further. It stopped looking down-at-heel and behind the times; it sprouted a theatre, a sports hall, a bright, retro-style uniform. Now, it is an academy and sucks in every middle-class child in a twenty-mile radius. In the prospectus, it still attributes all its success to its religious ethos.

2010 and Oldest One doesn't want to go to the Open Evening. It's at the Catholic school, and even at ten he is very against God. I don't really want him to go there either, but I do want a look at the buildings. I watched them go up from the park: a chapel, a rotunda, an atrium, an AstroTurf pitch; architect-designed, curved, coloured. Beautiful, the most beautiful school exteriors I've seen. I want to know if the interiors match up.

The neighbourhood believes that the Catholic Church paid for these glorious structures, but it's a bit more complicated than that. There was a Catholic middle school nearby, with generous grounds, in what is now a very desirable and expensive area of town. The middle school became redundant, and the buildings and playing fields were sold for development for a colossal sum. By law, this money had to be spent on another educational establishment, and the Church insisted it should be Catholic, and now, here it is, on the site of another redundant middle school. It's not, actually, in a great spot: only half a mile in either direction from two other comprehensives, while the other side of town has no secondary schools at all. But this is what the Church wanted, and under the new, Labour laws designed to encourage diversity, that is what we must have.

We enjoy the tour. The Cookery department makes great pumpkin muffins. The Art department has lovely windows. We are impressed by the library. We are less impressed by the History corridor – but with two lessons of Catholic RE every week here, and a compulsory GCSE in RE too, History must get squeezed. There are large crucifixes in every classroom, 3D ones with writhing Christ statues on top. There are notices about confession, and retreats. The Catholic Church is getting, I reckon, a lot of God for their investment, especially when you consider that much of this is missionary work. This isn't Birmingham or Liverpool – there really aren't many Catholics in our town. The school population is at least half Muslim, attracted, I assume, by the general anti-sex vibe.

Then, abruptly, the tour turns left and we are in the chapel. A solemn young man in a long robe explains that this is the most important place in the school. It's certainly gorgeous to look at: rounded, with heavy walls, embroidered hangings and flickering candles. I wonder if it would be such a bad thing for my son to go to the occasional service here. The priest is still talking; I look at the notice by the door. It's for a meeting of the Silver Ring Thing group. Silver Ring Thing is an American Christian youth movement. It encourages chastity before marriage, with a silver ring as a reminder. Ickily, in the States, fathers present daughters with the silver rings in mock wedding ceremonies.

My son is already scowling. The young priest asks him if he'd like to pray, and he shakes his head, mulishly, and sits on the end of a pew. The priest smiles and says soothingly that no one has to pray; they can simply think holy thoughts. The chaplaincy has a very wide brief here, and lots of extra help.

'Do you counsel students?' I ask. 'Do lay church people counsel students?'

'Yes,' says the priest. They are very lucky that way. In having so many lay people about.

'To run Silver Ring Thing?' I demand.

The priest agrees this is one of their programmes.

'A million dead of AIDS in Africa because of that sort of crap,' I say, still smiling.

'A million dead in Africa from AIDS,' says the priest, 'which is a sexually transmitted disease.'

'And,' I say, 'when a student comes to you and says he is gay, do you tell him it's a mortal sin?'

The priest says that his is a loving church and all sorts of confessions are welcome—

'But you think it's a mortal sin?'

In the long pause that follows, I hear my son being offered a tube of bubble mixture and a wand by a nice young woman.

'If you don't want to pray,' she is saying, 'you could just blow a bubble and think of Jesus.'

My son gets to his feet, appalled.

'We're just going,' I say. But she blows the bubble anyway.

'Yes,' says the priest, 'it is a mortal sin. And we do say so. That's the teaching of the church. But of course you don't have to choose to send your child here.'

We follow a trail of bubbles out of the door. It is true that I don't have to send my child here. But I also don't have a choice about paying, through taxation and my citizenship, for other children to be taught here, and I don't think anyone should be told that homosexuality is a sin in any state institution, or about Silver Ring Thing anywhere, on even the smallest bit of my money. I think we should agree on state values, things we all believe, and promulgate those. Religion should be for outside school only.

Besides, I think, as I lead my son out into the evening sun, watching the holy bubbles iridesce picturesquely round the stunning Art block, I may have a choice about this school, but I don't have a choice about the skew this school could give to my choice of school. This new, shiny, religious school could well attract the middle-class parents I see wandering anxiously around the site. They might enrol here, rather than at the other two nearby comprehensives, thus making the comps even less socially balanced than they were to start with. Things could easily get bad enough for me to have to eat humble pumpkin muffin and come crawling back in here to blow a bubble for Jesus, and I really don't want to do that, not after making such a righteous scene.

The Catholic school down the road does skew my choice of school, but not in the way I expected. The lovely buildings stay perfectly lovely, but over the next seven years its reputation does not solidify, it does not become over-subscribed, and its exam results are mediocre. After a few years, the original head leaves, and it is difficult to appoint another, because anyone above Assistant Principal level must be Catholic, and ours is not a Catholic town. Eventually, the school appoints internally, a newish teacher from a university background, someone with a PhD, but with no Vice Principal experience or record with disciplinary systems. Within eighteen months, the school is emptying, and there are children lighting small fires and smoking just yards from the gate. Ofsted come in and fail the place, singling management and governance out for blame. But there is very little that can be done; the Catholic community isn't large enough to supply new governors or a better head. In my school our excellent, tough Vice Principal is looking for a headship. She'd love to walk down the block and sort out the Catholic school, but she isn't just not Catholic; she's married to a woman. Now, our school fills to overflowing with children escaping from the Catholic school. Even the beautiful buildings start to look battered, litter accumulating against the pretty chapel.

Inside, the Catholic ethos and everything that goes with it – retreats, mass confessions, chapel, communal mass – are strong as ever. But the 'ethos' has not saved this school in the way it saved Acrostic High, perhaps because the 'ethos' was never the point in the first place, for either school. Acrostic High and many like it used Christianity to select its intake rather than to educate all the children. When Christ said, 'Suffer the little children,' he meant specifically the noisy, difficult ones who were being kept from the feast, not the baptized ones whose parents rang bells. Christ did not impose admission criteria; that is the work of man; and as men, voters, citizens, liberal humanists, people who believe in civic values and human rights, as ethical humans, we should make them fair.

About Prayer

Emily, Priya, and Kamal

Shakila asks me, 'Are you a Christian then, Miss?'

'No,' I say, 'but it's OK, you're safe with me, I'm a totally moral person.'

Shakila giggles. 'I know,' she says, 'but what's your religion?'

'Nothing,' I say. 'Humanism. No, wait a minute. Poetry. People. People saying poems. There you go.'

'OK, Miss,' says Shakila, smiling.

Dear Christian Emily, dear Muslim Priya, I do not scorn your faith. I do not scorn prayer, either. Schools are full of young people seeking to identify with something, so saying words together can be very powerful. I visited a transcendental meditation school once. No one had learned yogic flying, yet, but the meditation at the beginning of lessons certainly made everyone calm. *The prayers of all good people are good* is what Jim Burden's grandfather tells Jim in *My Antonia*, one of my favourite books about migration, as they watch Bohemian Mr Shimerda cross himself beneath their Protestant Christmas tree.

I don't think prayers have to be addressed to God, though, and definitely not to an established god. For example, in our school, Mr B induced a calm and prayerful atmosphere in 10E, that notorious zoo of a class, by teaching everyone to knit. I sometimes wonder if we could do the same across our whole school by issuing cotton reels and making French knitting compulsory after lunch. I already like our school motto: *Be the best you can be.* It may be a bit naive, but it is about us, and our personal responsibility, not God. The French knitting could be too, and we could murmur a personal affirmation as we wound the wool, something about being kind to each other, and allowing each other each day our daily differences, and forgiving small injuries as we ourselves would like to be forgiven, please, thank you, amen, bro. We have the motto and a shield on the school badge at present, but if the French knitting thing took off, we could easily add a bobbin.

And then our glorious, confounding, multicultural registers could be their own prayers.

> Osama, Mohamed, Jesus, Hope,
> Khatun, Swostika, Imam, Priest,
> Guarang, Shiney, Digweed, Hare,
> Awad, Mukahang, Zola, Mo.
> Kristos, Noor, Alkaida, Lunch.
> Fantasia, Bingy, Ulfat, Bird,

Urban, Allport, Garlick, Woods,
Princess, Zuleika, August, Best.
Timothy, Winter, Lord,
Amen.

Kamal's Paris

The Monday after the Paris attacks I have my Year 10s.
They are a noisy little group at the best of times, but this
morning they are impossible. Kara and Jade are curled in
their corner of the table, whispering about something. Izzat
crouches over his paper, drills a hole in it with his pen,
and yells, 'Get off me, man, get off!' in his loud, gravelly
voice when plump Mo sits down harmlessly beside him
and tries to unpack his bag.

They're a funny pair: Izzat so small and square and Afghan
with his big nose and premature moustache; Mo so rounded
and mellow and Pakistani with his long-lashed eyes and soft
glossy hair. On a good morning, the two of them will clasp
hands in greeting and stand still a moment: the manners of
a long-lost bazaar. Today, Mo answers Izzat's yells with a
long flow of resentful muttering, like a merchant justifying
his price. Now, they both appeal for support to Kamal, who
has loped in late, laid his bag in the very middle of the table
and himself out across his chair at maximum length, which
is, alarmingly, six foot two plus three inches of afro. Kamal
is Moroccan, and has a cool, difficult reputation in school.
But he likes poetry, and for me, after a couple of jokes, he
is usually both responsive and responsible. Not today.

'Man,' he says, 'oh man. I can't stop thinking about it.'

'He means the attacks,' says Mo, who makes knowing Kamal's thoughts his business. 'Miss! We ain't talked about anything else all weekend.'

'Been mad,' confirms Kamal, running his fingers through his afro. 'Crazy. Like, listening to the news all night.'

'Man!' says Izzat, incredibly loudly, banging his fist on the table. Jade looks up from her chat. Kara squeals.

'Like,' says Kamal, 'man. That's what people think *Muslim* means.' All three boys are Muslim, but different kinds. Mo is a mild sort of Shia, like many northern Pakistanis, Kamal a Moroccan *madhab*, which is a traditional, law-abiding sort of Sunni, and Izzat an Afghan Sunni, the religion of the Taliban.

'Yeah,' says Mo, 'that's the worst bit.'

'No man, the dead people is the worst bit,' says Izzat, 'and their families,' he adds, with feeling. He lost his dad in Afghanistan, I quickly remember. And a brother, I think. He despises the Taliban.

'Man,' says Mo, respectfully.

'Bro,' says Kamal. 'Oh man.'

'We ain't like that,' says Izzat. 'Miss. It ain't Muslim to kill people. It ain't the law. It's like the worst thing you can do. You know that, yeah?'

'It's totally, totally against the Koran,' says Mo, shaking his head.

'But people are going to think that about us, man,' says Kamal. 'Like, I'm a terrorist? Man. Like at the airport? The way they look at you. Man! I ain't never going there again. Like, never mind the airport. I ain't going to a concert. Or a club. I ain't never getting on the bus again.'

At this point, Kara unexpectedly bursts into tears, and the boys all look at her. 'That's terrible,' she squeals. 'Terrible, he can't get on a bus because people are like prejudiced! Everyone is!'

The boys pass hankies, thump her on the back. Kara howls more. Kara is plump, brown, shiny-haired, sentimental. I suspect she looks like the boys' mums. They are certainly enjoying the crying. Jade sighs, wrinkles her nose, looks at me meaningfully. She's right: this could go on for hours. My lesson plan is already a goner. Out the window.

I look round the room. It contains Muslims from five countries, one Hindu, a Filipino fundamentalist Christian, one transgender kid, two mixed race girls of no faith, two white kids, a Pole, and the full range of human skin colour. Fabulous.

'Not much prejudice in here,' I say. 'We could write a poem about it? Maybe? About Paris?'

So we do, and this is Kamal's. Subsequently, it becomes famous in the school and Kamal reads it from the podium at assembly, stepping down to many high-fives and cries of 'Man,' and 'You said it, bro.'

Bloody Paris
I heard the echo of the screams
of the innocent, of the witnesses,
of the bloody gruesome corpses.
The echo of blame.
The echo of ISIS.

Are they Muslims, that was an echo.

All Muslims are terrorists, that also was an echo.

Peace has no echo,

so there will never be silence.

Peace is universal and blood shouldn't be.

It probably has more abstract nouns and vague thinking than I would generally allow, but I think of this as a prayer, rather than a poem, so I make allowances. It's a prayer to multiculturalism; to Izzat and Mo and their friendship, all the more real for their disputes; to Kamal and his talent; and to Kara's muddled, sentimental, beautiful tears. Amen. *As-salamu alaikum, wa alaikum salam. The prayers of all good people are good.* (Mr Shimerda killed himself, in *My Antonia*, because he missed his country so.) Our Father. Bro. O, Man.

About Poverty, Art, and How
to Choose a School

Cheyenne, Darren, My Son, and Scarlett

What, demands Cheyenne, did I get my kids for Christmas?

Cheyenne and I are sitting on a sofa, eating breakfast. It's an Art Therapy project, an experiment for me, and I am not comfortable. I'm missing my protective desk, my pile of poems, my pens, but sofas is how they do things in here. 'Because I bet,' continues Cheyenne, 'I bet it was something really rubbish. People like you always get your kids rubbish things for Christmas. Book tokens.'

I pull a cushion onto my lap. I raise an eyebrow. I take a large bite of apple. Cheyenne is concentrated on the few morsels of chocolate croissant, snaffling up the scraps with small chapped hands.

'Do you know,' says Cheyenne, 'what I got for Christmas?' And I say, what an odd conversation, this is June.

'A BlackBerry,' says Cheyenne. 'Yeah. And a pair of boots, and an Xbox, and £200. All of that from my dad. And a pair of jeans, and a Burberry shirt. And a big box of make-up. Dior. So much stuff, he didn't even wrap it, it was in a big black bag. Like, *plummph*.' She gestures with her hands, the scale of the thing – right in the middle of the lounge.

'Right,' I say, as neutrally as I can. Kids quite often do tell you what they got for Christmas or birthdays, about their stuff, but usually small kids, at the end of the lesson, confidingly. Not fifteen-year-olds, not like this.

Cheyenne says: 'You didn't get your kids anything like that, did you? What did you get them?'

How does Cheyenne know I have kids? My back is up. If this were a classroom, I could just tell her she was inappropriate. If this were the Inclusion Unit, Miss B would do it. Here, I have to answer because we're on the damn sofa. I can't even remember what gifts I bought. 'Bikes,' I say eventually, 'this year, for the little ones.' Then, remembering the hunt for the right sort: 'Yes, bikes. Second hand. From eBay.'

EBay! Cheyenne's scorn is enormous. For the rest of the project, over several weeks, she starts each session by asking me if I got my kids something good yet, something new.

Then I notice Cheyenne in my sons' playground. Perhaps she has been there all the time: one of the teenagers who hang out on the benches and smoke and look at each other's phones. 'Hello, Miss,' she says in her deep hoarse voice, smiling her small smile. 'What about them scooters then, they new?'

So now Cheyenne knows where I live. Though she has probably always sort of known, in the same way I know where she lives: just ten minutes away from me, on the council estate. If she is a regular in our park, she must often walk through the narrow gap in the notorious 'Berlin

Wall' that separates the estate from the local conservation area and our block of pretty, privately owned Victorian houses. The wall is notorious because it is so ugly – fifteen foot of seventies brick – and because it has no other purpose than to separate the rich from the poor.

Of course, as a nice liberal person, I disapprove of this wall. On the other hand, I rarely go through the gap myself. I speed up, in fact, when I am obliged to cycle through the estate. Not that it's ugly; on a sunny day, with a glow on its interlocking crescents of brick houses and front gardens, it reminds me of my childhood Ladybird books, the ones which showed 1960s family life in Technicolor: Father in a short-sleeved shirt, Mother in a buttoned yellow dress, a dog to walk in the bright green park. Aspiration, circa 1959.

Or Utopia, circa 1901: the recreation ground, the large, purpose-built, deco-style primary school, the (disused) library; this is what Booth and Rowntree and the great Victorian social reformers wanted for working people. I imagine explaining to them why these spacious, solid houses now mean 'poor' and the narrow, poorly built Victorian streets they deplored currently mean 'rich'.

Mr Booth, Mr Rowntree, it is hard to say, but, if you live here, easy to know. Rich people drive past the estate shopping centre to the Waitrose a mile away; only poor people use the Spar, where the prices, oddly, are higher. Everyone rich knows not to walk their dog in the recreation ground; everyone poor knows this shit pool is theirs. Only the poor send their kids through the pretty deco gate of the spacious council estate primary school, because everyone rich knows the results are bad. There's a faith school for rich people – Victorian, poky, successful, and overcrowded – just down the road.

Mr B, Mr R, you spent so much time recording your society, had so much faith in writing it down. If you wrote down the council estate, now, you would record that here, there are families that have not worked for three generations, since the car plant closed; and that the contrast between my children's and Cheyenne's prospects in life is of proportions you still recognize: of nineteenth-century, Princess and Match Girl size. Nevertheless, Cheyenne's boast about Christmas presents is not a tragic fantasy, and she is not lying about her BlackBerry or her Burberry shirt, for this is poverty in the twenty-first century, and it's complicated.

For a start, the breadline, or, rather, the lack of one. There is a great deal of work in our town, work which continued even in the depths of the 2008 recession; we have two universities, three huge hospitals, bio-tech, publishing, tourism, and even some heavy industry. Because the car plant that closed to such disastrous effect thirty years ago in a blaze of strikes and violence actually quietly reopened shortly afterwards. It is now much more successful than it ever was, but is also smaller, foreign owned, and staffed by robots and a tiny number of highly skilled engineers supplemented by agency workers on minimum wage or lower. The hospitals, bio-tech, and other industries divide on the same lines: a small number of highly paid, highly skilled jobs; a larger number of agency workers doing menial jobs on semi-legal rates. The unions are broken, and there is no incentive for anyone to raise the bottom level of pay because the town benefits from a steady flow of young immigrants willing to accept any wage, and also from part-time workers subsidized by state tax credits.

Housing is rather similar: our small brick house is now worth three times what we paid for it because the large number of very rich people in town, including many who commute daily to London, has forced up house prices to near-London levels. Private rents have risen in tandem, to the point where we all assume, in school, that a thirty-year-old teacher will live like a student in a single room. The social housing in the city is available only to the very poorest, such as Cheyenne's family, and is being continually chipped away by the Right to Buy.

All of this means it is very difficult for Cheyenne's mother, for example, to step out of living on benefits. She has three children and receives benefits and tax credits for them; in order to have more real income than she currently receives from the state, especially in housing benefit, she would have to earn more than £50,000 a year. She can't do this, because she has no education, so the smartest way for her to pay for her children's needs is either to be unemployed, or, better, to do a legal, part-time job and claim tax credits, and subsidize it with an illegal job, of which there are many in the city, on the side. If Cheyenne's absent father, meanwhile, were to move back in, and get a legal job, or even start making regular declared parental payments, the family would undoubtedly be poorer; he can give his family much more by staying out, working illegally, and contributing uncounted sums of cash and stuff in black bags.

Cheyenne almost certainly does have more consumer goods than my children, in the same way that she has more calories and less nutrition; more cash and less financial security. In the estate, too, she may well have a larger bedroom in a bigger house; but already she has far less chance of ever owning a home of her own. It is sharp of her to have noticed my kids in the park, with their hand-me-down trousers and large vocabularies, and chosen them to envy. It shows that she has noticed that something is amiss here, that they have something she does not; that my second-hand bicycle has a quality which makes it a rich person's present, while her own black bag of goods is a poor gift, and that she and her father have somehow been palmed off with something, a lie about value and status, choice and freedom, and the way things work.

And I fear that Cheyenne has decided that I, in my worn tweed jacket, with my dubious, in-between, first-name status, am the ideal person to explain this conundrum, or, at least, make the injustice explicit so she can liberate some of her anger about it. For Cheyenne has taken to tracking me round school, and she really does have 'anger issues'; I hear about them all the time. Her outbursts are famous because they are so pungent and so personal. Mostly, I notice, they are targeted at women, and have something to do with what their kids have.

The year I meet Cheyenne, all three of my children are at the C of E primary school she didn't go to, the most middle-class one in the area. It is full of the children of people like me: highly educated, often freelance, living on relatively low incomes. Therapists, yoga teachers, editors, academics: all tucked into small houses with over-stuffed cupboards and wonky IKEA kitchens. Most of them, like me, went to private schools ourselves, because, when we were children in the seventies and eighties, most middle-class children did, and most middle-class parents could afford to send them. Now, in the noughties, we send our children to state schools; partly because we are left-leaning, and partly because private schools have become vastly more expensive, well beyond the reach of teachers and academics, let alone writers and yoga teachers. It is part of our surprising disinheritance; brought up in large houses by parents who taught us to look to a more equal society, we find ourselves living in cupboards, with a new class of the super-rich lording it over us. Still, we cling to our education and our politics; we are nice lefties yet.

Nice leftie middle-class parents are in theory an asset to a school because they bring high expectations and because their children are usually quick to learn and easy to teach. With any luck, we might become governors, start an after-school club, help. I do see parents like this, but in our primary school we are also often fusspots, uselessly at loggerheads with the teachers. We fuss because our expectations are unsettled. We don't have personal experience of large classes, multiculturalism, dinner money, and it disconcerts us. We want a school like we went to ourselves, but not: more sport, but no exclusion from sport; more languages, more selection, more setting, yet also more equality.

The more time I spend in the Inclusion Unit, the harder

I find it to sympathize when my fellow primary parents murmur about special needs – why is their child not deemed to have any, when he is so very good at maths – and about behaviour, for though their children are scruffy, and swear, they still don't want them sitting next to the one with real meltdowns, the one who hits. They fuss about 'cultural exclusion' in a C of E assembly, yet band tightly together and never ask a child in hijab home for tea. I hate it, above all, when they mutter about the teachers, who are not as educated as they are, have not read enough, use language coarsely, are not of their class. 'It must have been nice for you to have a clever person like me to teach,' I hear Isaac observe to the faithful and hard-working Mrs D as he leaves for private school.

And now Oldest One is in Year 6, choosing a secondary school, and we fussy parents are working ourselves into a frenzy over the choice. Where shall we send our delicate, clever, between-class sprogs? Which school should be so lucky as to receive them? Where indeed? The line-up, as I see it, hasn't changed much since I was a trainee teacher here, twenty-five years previously. There are the private schools: two highly academic; two less so but sporty; two to pick up the sensitive ones; one for those who can't spell. They are famously successful, most of these schools, and in our rich little city many children go to them – about a quarter of the children who live inside the ring road. But they are unaffordable, and seem too, to both my husband and I, to be unrecognizable as the sort of school we went to – repulsively pressured, in fact, and horribly socially exclusive.

Then there are the state schools, impoverished already, of course, by the loss of that 25 per cent. There is the famously good comp, and the good comp, both defended by a thicket of estate agents' boards – but we live too far away to get into either of them. Near us is the Catholic school, the decent comp, and, nearest of all, my school, the one with Cheyenne and the Inclusion Unit, with Miss B and Miss T and Miss A and its bright, brand-new head – the school I am already beginning to love. But: 'You couldn't send him there,' said my nearest neighbour. 'So cute, and with his little French horn. Might as well put a sign saying "Hit me" round his neck. The problem,' she went on, 'is that that school has become a sort of bin. All the really bad kids at our school?' (She has good children at the good comp.) 'They send them down there.'

Alas, poor Oldest One, by virtue of age pioneer of the family: my bookish, quiet, beautiful boy. He must walk first, with his wide eyes wide, into adolescence, into a school where the kids are full height, where they have bosoms and beards; just as he has obediently walked first, with careful, stilted steps, into every nursery, drop-in centre, park, friendship. Now he must also go, the first of his family on either side for a thousand generations, as Neil Kinnock said of the Kinnocks, to a state secondary. Can we really add to that that he must go to the least desired school in the neighbourhood, the one on the wrong side of the Wall? The choosing year, I often seem to find myself in school standing at the bottom of a staircase listening to the harsh noise of descending teenagers and looking for my son's peers.

Because if I believe that the class divide is bad and that schooling is a vital chance to dissolve it, if I deplore the Wall, then I should send my son here, to our local school. But: 'This isn't a comprehensive school,' says Miss B, kind and frank and frustrated. 'It doesn't have a top. You can look at the stats, cut them any way you like. We don't get the middle-classes. We don't get the brighter kids.' She speaks only the truth. Nationally, about 40 per cent of pupils at the end of the final year of primary school are Level 5 in Maths and English, cleverer than expected. In our school's intake, it is fewer than 10 per cent. Nationally, 20 per cent are Level 3, that is, not at the 'expected level', not really ready for secondary; for us, it is 40 per cent. My son is Level 6.

On paper, I remind myself, on paper: many of our students arrive late, have hidden qualities, blossom. Here, lumbering down the stairs with an enormous school bag, is Mattias, the strangely brilliant Hungarian, behind him some serious-looking Poles. And here is Emily, the pastor's daughter, my very favourite student, with her precious violin, the only one for miles. She looks OK. And, here, actually, are the famously brainy Year 9 twins, chatting to each other, carrying briefcases, neatly combed. I know their mother. She is from my side of the Wall and believes you should send your child to the local school, no compromises. Her boys look fine. But there're two of them: a portable peer group. What if my son came alone, without a single primary school friend? Already, I know that one best friend is going to a private school; another to a state school outside the ring road, three bus rides away, a good school, a white school.

Though this is a class divide, not a racial one. I don't fear the Somali and Ghanaian and Afghan kids thundering past me in hijabs and *dishdashas* and diamanté baseball caps – and I don't believe my middle-class friends do, either. In England, social classes fear each other more than racial groups do, because that is where the history is, the abuse. I fear Darren, looming out from behind Mo and Imam. Darren from the Art Project. Darren, also from the estate. Enormous Darren with his belly and huge hands and huge shout and his eyes darting everywhere for offence. Darren with the father and older, even larger, brother in prison.

And I fear Cheyenne, popping up beside me again, asking about my children, asking about my shoes. Cheyenne and her mean mouth, leaking insults at Emily, who doesn't seem to hear. I fear Cheyenne and the class hate she carries with her. I know she has a point, and it's not her fault; on the other hand, it isn't my kid's fault, either.

If the problem, as Cheyenne points out, is not actual money but habits of mind, not access to school but the wish to learn, what should we do about it? How do we, as a school or as a nation, educate Cheyenne, get her to adopt middle-class habits such as reading, homework, and long-term ambition, without alienating her from her family? How do you induce her to go through the difficulties and deferred gratifications of studying when everyone around her would say that did not work for them?

There are a lot of suggestions around, for this is the late noughties, and the educational plight of disadvantaged children is beginning to be clarified as their underperformance emerges, unchanging and solid as a rock, from the new, swirling floods of computerized school data. Mossbourne Academy in Hackney has just released its first, stunning set of GCSE results and the papers are full of the remarkable effects of strict uniform, silent corridors, and – this seems to pique every journalist's attention – silent ping pong at the beginning of the day, on a motley bunch of Hackney kids. (Actually, Mossbourne did a lot of nurture groups and reading recovery too, but that doesn't make the headlines.) The latest thinking is: merciless challenge, rigid boundaries, drastically raised expectations.

A wave of new academies is breaking across the country in a foam of shiny, man-made blazers, this being the easiest part of the Mossbourne recipe to imitate. Miss B goes for an interview in one of them and tells the new head about the IU. He leans back in his new leather chair and says, 'Touchy feely understanding? What about a bit of challenge?' It takes three years for this delightful individual's school to fail its Ofsted and for him to be ignominiously sacked, but longer for his words to leave Miss B, for her standards were always high and always challenging. It's just that the IU acknowledged that for some kids, very simple things were challenging.

Miss T, though, Cheyenne's English teacher, is Mossbourne in her own diminutive, high-heeled person. She is as famous through the school as Miss B, though they are regarded as rather opposite phenomena. Miss B teaches the whole person, then her subject; Miss T is resolutely only interested in English Literature. Miss B understands everything about the students' background and always bears it in mind; Miss T proceeds as if that background did not exist. Miss B is warm, jokey, and available all hours; Miss T is glamorous and terrifying, and delivers her elegant, exhausting lessons in a classroom laid out in rows, dishing out detentions for yawning. Students run to Miss B in tears; but stagger out of Miss T's classroom as the bell rings, clutching their foreheads as if some fundamental rearrangement had taken place. Both Miss B and Miss T, interestingly, are working-class girls who misbehaved at school. Both are living proof that there is not one single path to being an excellent teacher, getting extraordinary results, or being very loved – neither silent ping pong nor nurture groups. Both get on with me, but not with each other, like the opposing magnets they are.

But they are both keen on my new lunchtime Poetry Group; Miss B for the personal development, and Miss T for the literature. And both suggest it to Cheyenne, and Cheyenne comes, comes regularly, and interrupts the cosy camaraderie I was beginning to establish, by staring at us all impassively with one pencilled eyebrow raised, rarely writing anything at all. What is she even doing there?

Perhaps, says Miss B, perhaps Cheyenne just wants to come on the trip. Because we've booked a day out of school, at a literary festival. Trips, Miss B has taught me, are a huge deal for a kid like Cheyenne. Because here is an effect of deprivation that is far worse than generally imagined: poor children don't travel. Over the years I work at our school, I take several into the historic city centre who have never been there before, though it is only twenty minutes away on the bus. It is as if there are real walls round the edge of the council estate, with checkpoints. Cheyenne has never, she confides during a lesson on Thomas Hardy, been on a train.

Miss B took the IU out frequently, taking advantage of every free offer going. Once, we took the kids to Somerset House in London, and somehow I got left in the top gallery, the one that's like a sumptuous sitting room, with Vikki and Dave. Vikki was keen on the images of ladies in hats; Dave was in thrall to the surfaces of the oil paintings, the clear slicks of colour without so much as a brush mark. Together, they sat on a red plush seat and held hands, in a room filled with the floating light of the Thames, and looked at their reflections in the gilt-framed mirror. It felt like a moment of joy and expansion, a whole new idea, the sudden abolition of the Wall.

On the other hand, I remember taking my Essex students to Cambridge, their visible unease among the beautiful buildings I thought would attract them. 'They was too much for us, Kate,' said Zoe, who I thought ought to apply to King's, 'you can feel them looking down on you.' Super-brainy Zoe, who explained to me that the reason she was finding it difficult to plan for university was because she had never met anyone, other than teachers, who had actually been there. Zoe, who refused to apply to Cambridge, and went, despite my warnings of green wellies, to Exeter, and rang me from a pay phone the first week saying help, all the girls here have been abroad, and none of them can cook. Lovely Zoe, who always had a point.

But, says Miss B, looking at the festival invite, with kids like Cheyenne you have to be resilient.

Miss T says, with kids like Cheyenne you must offer them the best. The very best. Like Shakespeare.

And I say, OK.

And so we put Cheyenne's name on the list, pass it under the raised eyebrows of her form teacher and the Deputy Head, and indeed, on the festival bus, our hearts swell with pride when we turn the corner of the road and show Cheyenne our destination: a real, a top-drawer, an honestly Jacobean castle, golden as a fresh-baked cake on its very own shimmering silver plate of a moat. And what does she think of that! She chews a lock of hair, her eyes blacker than ever. 'Nah,' she says. 'That ain't beautiful. Why did you say it was going to be beautiful? It ain't beautiful at all.'

Worse, when she is there, Cheyenne and some other students disrupt a session with a young writer, a beautiful and clever young woman who has given up her time to talk pro bono to disadvantaged children about her witty, clever, top-drawer, silver-plate book. I speak to the writer afterwards, tearful by the moat, and try to console her, but I can see that I am not succeeding. She has been humiliated, ripped into like a young teacher in training. Cheyenne has sprayed her with the full force of her class hatred, and she can't wipe it off. She won't give up her time again.

So is the castle beautiful, as it seemed to Miss B, or just an embodiment of money, privilege, and exclusion, as it seemed to Cheyenne? Is King's College Chapel beautiful or 'just looking down on us', as it seemed to Zoe? And if they aren't, is even poetry beautiful, as it seems to me; or Shakespeare an essential good, as it seems to Miss T; or classical music a spiritual force, as it seems to be already, so powerfully, to my son?

I am not a relativist. I believe the castle is essentially beautiful; not for the rich family that lives in it, but for its shape, its placement in the landscape, its stonework, its mullions, its gardens – each of which represents hundreds and thousands of acts and thoughts of men who were not rich; each of which is a work of art. I believe in poetry and Shakespeare in the same way some people believe in God. I take Bach, by extension, on trust. Cheyenne does not disturb that belief essentially – but she has put her chapped finger with its elaborate nail extension once again squarely on one of my self-doubts: whether I am a posh do-gooder, a Victorian lady on a mission who has not noticed that her message is obscured by her person, and the injustices of class which she embodies.

Sometimes, I can see that question on the faces of the school staff too. If I want to work among them, I should be more like them: more a teacher than a writer. I should be like Miss A, who graduated from Cambridge thirty years ago and has done nothing ever since except teach uncompromisingly excellent lessons; she has shown more children the beauty of poetry than any visiting writer ever could. I should be more like Mr H, the geography teacher, who takes minibus after minibus out of school to show children in hijabs the beautiful and ancient things of the English countryside – the White Horse, Stonehenge, Durdle Door – with the same indefatigable patience that he later uses to swim the Channel, backstroke. Above all, if I want to show Cheyenne that I see her as equal to my children, I should send my child to school alongside her, however afraid I might be.

Miss T says: it isn't treating Cheyenne as an equal if you make exceptions for her. That's a double standard, a low expectation. If she behaved badly on that trip, you should report it.

So I make a report of Cheyenne to her form teacher. Miss C listens and nods. She is an extremely patient woman and Cheyenne takes up a lot of her time. Cheyenne, she says, is particularly difficult right now because she isn't well. The problem, well, one of the problems, is her teeth. The molars on both sides of her mouth are so profoundly rotted and infected that they have to be removed under general anaesthetic. She has to have, at fifteen years old, false teeth. In fact, Cheyenne is going into hospital next week and will be absent for Poetry Group, if that is any consolation to me.

It isn't much of a consolation to me. It isn't much consolation to her form teacher, either; you can tell by the way she is whispering, her eyes down. She is a mother, I am a mother, and we both have our hands over our mouths. We are holding down the thought: what sort of mother did that? Never took her daughter to the dentist, not once, never brushed her teeth? Because Cheyenne has been entitled to free dental care since the day she was born, just as she has been entitled to free swimming pool entry, and library books, and never used those, either.

Oh, Mr Booth, Mr Rowntree, poverty has survived every

reform you could have imagined, and a few you couldn't. Poverty is stronger than plumbing, stronger than medicine, stronger than art. Poverty is stamped through Cheyenne like letters in a stick of rock, manifesting itself in her rotting, nineteenth-century mouth.

The teeth absence lasts much longer than a week, and Cheyenne comes back to Poetry Group just once, for the session before Christmas. She upsets everyone by pouring contempt on the Edwin Morgan poem I have brought in to show them – that ain't good, that's stupid, you can't see that, no, no you can't understand it, it's shit ain't it. Then, when I try to smooth things over by showing her a typed-up version of one of her own poems, she becomes apoplectic because I have changed 'was' to 'were'. She accepts nothing I have to say about the subjunctive. She shouts. I give her her work and ask her to leave, which, surprisingly, she does.

And soon after that, she leaves school and goes to live in a nearby town with the dad of the black bag. In the staffroom, my colleagues recount pleasant conversations they have had with her, say that really, she was on the turn, on the verge of making a breakthrough. They seem genuinely regretful. Not me. I find the spaces between buildings easier to cross, now there is no risk of Cheyenne leaping in front of me, or shouting quotes from my Wikipedia page after me in her deep hoarse voice. I find it easier to see my son here.

The new head decrees choirs (you cannot say that she does not believe in the arts) and I watch Miss B integrate Darren in hers, and witness him actually come back into school, after hours, for a concert. He stands next to Andrew, a tall Ghanaian boy, and the two of them step forward together to sing the bottom notes in 'Bohemian Rhapsody', to wild applause.

But afterwards, leaving the building, I hear him nag at Emily and her violin. 'Doesn't it bother you?' I ask. She tucks her little instrument into its furry nest. 'He can't play it, can he?' she says, and clicks shut the case, and picks up the handle, and smiles.

Our school doesn't have an orchestra. The good comp does, and the private schools drip with grand pianos. If my son went to the private school he could play in chamber groups. But if he went to my school, he could carry his French horn in for his lesson, as Emily does her violin, and then there would be a French horn in the school corridor, it would exist. That's a patrimony, a gift, as Emily's fiddle is a gift to the school – as Emily is in general, and the brainy twins too: asking the penetrating questions in every lesson, never failing in good manners and intelligent, tempered enthusiasm, always getting the teacher's joke, hauling up the grade point average, constantly raising the bloody tone. Maybe I should be thinking of what my son could bring to the school, as well as what he could take, about his patrimony as well as his entitlement. After all, looking at Cheyenne, he has had quite a lot of stuff, and quite a lot of luck, already.

I am standing in the English corridor, waiting for the bell to ring. I'm early, as I often am. I like listening to the sounds of the lessons: Year 10, I surmise. Here is Miss A, telling Set 1 about racism in *Of Mice and Men* in her elegant, clear, unafraid sentences, so much the most interesting thing they will hear all day; Miss B's room rumbling with happy giggles as Set 3 act out the scene with Curley's wife. Miss T's is nearly silent except for the click of her heels. Then there is a disruption, and a door is flung open, and the immense Darren flings himself out of her classroom. He leans against a wall, puts his hands flat against it, and shakes.

He seems to shake the building. He seems to shake the air. I have never seen anything quite like it. I remember what Miss B told me: that Darren comes from a family where all the older men are in prison, that he was witness to the murder of a child when he was only five years old himself. That must be what makes anger like this: an emotion big as weather.

After a while, I ask him if he is all right. After all, I do know him. We ate toast on a sofa together. For a minute, I think he will hit me, then he puts his hands in his pockets. 'Yeah,' he says, 'yeah, Miss.' He gestures down the corridor. 'I am all right. I got anger issues, Miss.'

Then the bell rings, and, as the other kids come belting out of the classrooms, the noise rising like water, he goes back in. Through the glass pane of the door I see him sit down, and Miss T put a paper on the desk in front of him, and his head bend to the desk. A test – probably for GCSE, probably Steinbeck. Miss T, and the school, and Steinbeck, and Darren himself, are going to face down his anger, anger big as Cheyenne's anger, bigger, and he will probably write down how much he likes the book, and the scenes about hopelessness, poverty, tenderness, and violence, because probably, he does.

Later, I help Miss A take a display down from her wall, and she shows me a piece Cheyenne wrote for her, a response to World War I poems, a letter from a woman left behind. It says all the usual things, the mixture of cliché and anachronism – but she has written each word carefully, in ink pen, and scorched the paper, to make it look old, and painted a watercolour poppy in the corner, quite well. And in the middle, between 'Sammy says you are a great role model' and 'Love you forever' is the line, 'I think of you in the slow dusk, and all down the street the women pull down their blinds.' None of the other pieces of work has this borrowing from Owen, so I think Cheyenne might have liked his poem, really.

And if she liked that, then perhaps she might have liked the golden castle, really. Perhaps she even liked the poem she so scorned, the Edwin Morgan one, which, come to think of it, was about Christmas, and presents. About a trio of young people coming down the street with a new guitar, happy in their lives, full of love: *Orphean sprig! Melting baby! Warm Chihuahua! / The vale of tears is powerless before you.* I wonder what it is like to see that castle or to read that poem when you come, in fact, from the vale of tears and will be going back there in the evening. And perhaps, I think, perhaps – it is a chilly little thought, because I never liked her, never gave her a genuine smile, not as Miss B did, never believed in her intellectual potential, not as Miss A did – perhaps Cheyenne actually liked me. Perhaps her rage at Edwin Morgan, the young writer, the castle, my children's parcels, was the measure not of her hate, but of her love.

'Your school doesn't have a ski trip,' says one of the mothers at my primary. 'The other comprehensive has a ski trip. I do think that's important, a ski trip.'

This is crazy talk. But choosing a school is making all the Year 6 parents crazy. Of course it is. This is the most political choice we will ever make, far beyond voting, and it involves our children, whom we love beyond reason. It makes it worse that the terror of what we are doing has made passive-aggressive hypocrites of us all. The parents who are sending their kids to private school are telling everyone who will listen that it is because of their child's special needs: because he/she is so good/bad at Maths, so good/bad at socialization, so terribly in the middle that no one will notice him/her, and we the parents who do not have the money to consider private school are agreeing with them loudly about their child's weakness, and deploring them afterwards, and cheering secretly when they fail the entrance exam, which, most satisfactorily, some of them do.

One of my friends even cuts another from her social circle when she announces their intention to send their son to private school. I quite admire this but don't do it myself; I listen to the separate rants instead. The private-school husband is furious; he says that anyone could send their child privately, it's like taking out another mortgage, and it's a highly moral thing to do because you are saving the state money. But you are buying a slice of unfair privilege, I fail to say. But your parents are paying, I don't remark. And anyway, my son loves your son, I definitely don't say. Your son expands my child's world with his funniness and social confidence and brains, and you and your wife run the orchestra, and help him with his French horn. You are taking something away from the community when you withdraw your child, I don't say. Your patrimony, his patrimony. And you're hurting my boy. (Never say that.) Don't take anything away from my child, no one says. Because that would be crazy, and they will, anyway.

Not that these parents would have picked my school even if they were picking a state school. No one in the primary is choosing my school; the place is epically, record-breakingly under-subscribed, and the reason seems to be ski trips, or rather, what underlies the ski trip: class. I turn to the only parent I know who stands outside the English class system. Mamie is from Alabama, and, as she puts it, black folks don't ski. Her son is my son's most fluent and confident friend, and her husband used to be a teacher; together, we can do this. With this family, my husband and I take a careful tour of the school. We talk to Miss A and Miss B, and the new head, who impresses us. We look at the library. We read the school newsletter, not about a ski trip but another of Mr H's wheezes: 'Chanelle and Rabiah enjoy the River Windrush', with a marvellous picture of a round girl in a hijab and a rounder girl without, grinning ear to ear in the mud.

Mamie likes the school: the ethnic mix, the Head's

commitment, the firm discipline, the go-ahead attitude. Her husband appraises the timetabling and the staff system and sees that it is good. My husband sees a place where books are loved and his child will be cared for. And so we make our joint decision: our sons are going to their nearest local school. Shockwaves rock our tiny community. No one, I am told later, talked about anything else in the playground for a full three weeks.

Are we moral grandstanding? Taking risks with our children's future? Just being crazy? It feels like all those things. My son at eleven is blond and angelic, Mamie's son curly-haired and preternaturally handsome, and this, from a short story written by their classmate a few years later, is how they appear to the rest of them when they enter their new school gates:

Louis and Richard entered the school grounds at the same time. They did not know anyone from the school. We knew them though. We looked at their leather bags and their ironed shirts, and we saw their sheltered childhoods and their days spent inside. We looked at their shining hair and their polished shoes, and their eager faces, and saw the equally eager looks of their parents, as they looked at the average grades for the school, and the false advertisements claiming that the school was a 'peaceful learning environment' and that 'your children will survive the first day'. They had no idea. Louis and Richard trotted into the building, like pigs into a slaughterhouse.

Cheyenne, a few years later, some texts from Miss T:

> *On the bus . . . and guess who's behind me –*
> *Cheyenne.*
> *Has she recognized you?*
> *Boom ah Boom – the devil may say. Boom ah Boom –*
> *you left any way.*
> *Excuse me?*
> *Cheyenne's music. Very loud.*
> *Ah. You going to say hi?*
> *I don't think so – too scary.*
> *How does she look?*
> *Like Banquo's ghost.*
> *Eyeliner run? Hair bleach?*
> *No. Like the saddest, angriest person in the world.*
> *Like she wants to destroy the world. Like the world*
> *deserves it.*

My son, a few years later.

He's just fine. So is Mamie's son. Their year group was so small and so wildly mixed that being middle-class counted as just another odd minority identity, and they were never bullied. The boy who wrote the story, an exceptionally bright, mathsy, oddball Pole, was their dearest friend, and they all mooched about together through Year 11, the tall, sardonic ones. Even the French horn was a hit; my son played it with the bass guitar, Emily's fiddle, and a chorus of girls in the House Music contest and won. Afterwards, several people admiringly asked how you turned it on.

As for their brains (for they were both very clever boys), they were for the most part sweetly, naively admired. Before GCSE Maths, my son was passed round his class to hug, 'so the smarts would rub off'. In the classroom, true, things did not go always as fast as they might like, so they learned to read for themselves and ask for more. In Music, my son had lots of private instrument lessons. And as for the exam results, they did exactly as well as they ought to have for such well-supported, able lads; as well, in fact, as such kids statistically almost always do, whatever school they go to. For my son, this meant a full hand of A* GCSE grades, and it is hard to do better than that.

What they received at school: those grades, a special card from Faroq entitling them to free minicab rides in exchange for all the help in Maths, the ability to knit, an acquaintanceship with kids from every corner of the globe, and the confidence that if they walked across any rough park in town, late at night, and were approached by a hooded gang, it would probably just be Mo and Izzat, saying hi. What they gave: their own oddity in the rich mix of the school, their Maths coaching, their articulate voices in class, their academic demands, their parents' informed labour, their high grades to spike the stats, their evident wellness and cheer to act as advertisement for other parents, their part as pioneers in a huge change that saw the school, in the four years before my younger children went too, become the popular comp, the over-subscribed one, the one it was safe to go to with your French horn.

And one other thing they got: the knowledge that they had something to give – a patrimony – as well as something to take, from the communities they joined. They were very lucky.

Darren, a few years later.

We attend a school performance of *Bugsy Malone.*

I like musicals. I like the simplicity of the form, the clarity of the storytelling, the way that populism, the steady demands of the peanut gallery, has smoothed them to lozenges, sweet in the mouth, easy to swallow. If there is a Wall between low art and high art then the musical is the gate.

And so is the school play. Nothing is a more powerful tool for building a community, nothing enables and frames and excites children more than an ensemble piece of theatre. The first artistic writing of my own I ever dared to do was to cut *Oklahoma!* into a shape that could fit a cast of girls, and the ancient Music teacher's son, aged forty-two, singing Curly. It was great. No lyric poem I have completed has made me happier than cutting *A Midsummer Night's Dream* down to the right size for Year 6, and magically halving and doubling the Mechanicals' lines to create a troupe of female players. When children step forward to sing, I cry, even if I don't know the child, even if it's just 'Happy Birthday'.

This musical suits me perfectly. A scratch performance, all ensemble and no stars, all vim and few costumes, wobbling flats, last-minute cast changes, a stand-out performance from a small black boy who rarely speaks, day to day. My son is on the piano, conscientiously plinking. His lines have been cut because no one could persuade him to speak audibly, but his ability to string notes together is widely admired. My husband and I, meanwhile, are not quite the only white people in the audience, but we are the only tall white people, the only ones in collars. Sitting next to us are two women in vest tops and leggings, with orange hair and broken noses, and vast, tattooed arms. It is hard to say their age, or if one is older than the other, but the small, shaven-headed children they have with them call one 'Mum' and one 'Nan'. Three songs into the play, our row of seats shakes and Darren, who seems to have grown to six foot five, wobbles in. So this is his family; this, not the trilby hats and splurge guns on stage, is what a criminal's family looks like: a gangster's moll, a murderer's unlucky son.

'Hello,' I say, 'hello, Darren. Well done on your GCSEs.' Because he got five, mostly thanks to Miss B, though he rent the school nearly in two and set a new record for the hammer throw in the process. He has a job with the council, caretaking. It's a miracle.

He nods acknowledgement. 'I come to see Scarlett,' he says, indicating the stage. His sister, two sisters down. She's doing surprisingly well, as is the sister older than her. Neither of them seems as vulnerable, or as angry, as Darren. Perhaps, I think – because he has put on more weight, his bulky arms overshadowing my seat – perhaps he is the shock absorber of the family, and it is he who has allowed Scarlett to get this far, to play Smokey Priscilla in a flapper dress, glittery headband pulled down over her ears. She is a knock-kneed, hollow-hipped, pale little creature, not well named. Her lines are inaudible, but she likes to dance, her arms round her friends. At the end of the song, her family don't seem to know how to clap. They look around, puzzled and anxious, as if they will be told off.

'She's very good,' I tell the mother. 'Scarlett, she's great in that part.' And the mother blushes like a girl. I tell her that is my son, at the piano, and then she says he is amazing for his years. And we both clap for the encore and go our separate ways. And that is the best we can manage. I think we're doing well.

About Prizes

Phillip and Tanya

I am having coffee with Jeannie when texts start to come in from Miss T. She has moved schools but has not lost the habit of confiding her outrage on educational issues. She is particularly articulate when irritated.

Prizes: reads the text. *There is an English prize here, for Year 11. I want it to go to Phillip, because he is top in English. Everyone else wants to give it to Tanya, 'because she has really turned it around this year'. I am not making this up. T.*

I show this text to Jeannie, who laughs her head off. Her daughter is exceptionally good at Maths, but each year her school prize goes to someone who has 'made progress'.

'Which really devalues the prize,' observes Jeannie. 'Because, you know, in Maths everyone knows your marks. It's numbers! There are the Maths Challenges and all that, and Annie is always top by a yard. So the kid who did get the Maths prize over Annie knows that he is really just getting a pat on the head. They know it's Annie's prize, really. To say nothing of the unabashed, total, shameful sexism round the whole thing. Cos it's always a boy – it's like they are correcting some injury done to the collective male pride.'

'Ping,' says my phone. Miss T is clearly having a rough meeting. *Phillip,* texts Miss T, *has white skin and bulbous eyes and has two listening-to-Miss expressions. One with his head back and a finger pressed in each eye; one with his head down, writing frantically in his spidery handwriting. I love Phillip. But they say he can't have the prize because everyone already knows he's good. How do I explain?*

This makes Jeannie cross. 'Teachers underestimate how hard it is to be clever,' she says. 'Annie never said so, but it's tough. She goes to school every day as the nerdy girl with spots. She works bloody hard, on her own, mostly. She pays a price. She's never going to get the popularity prize. Where's her Maths prize?'

My son, too. He went all the way through school hardworking and modest, especially about his accelerated ability in Maths. He never boasted, he always helped his neighbour, he did the work and more work and accepted his nerdy status and laughed about it and he wanted the Maths prize very much in compensation. Fortunately, he mostly got it, but the times he failed to hurt him surprisingly much, however much I told him, much as I knew he understood, about his less lucky classmates. 'It's called the Maths Prize,' he says. 'Not the Nice Prize. Or the Turnaround Prize. I can't turn around, I'm going in the right direction already.'

'Last week,' says Jeannie, 'George came back from school really upset.' (George is Annie's much younger brother.)

'They had these places in the carnival float, and Miss F said they were behaviour prizes, for the best behaviour in the next three weeks. So George has been splitting himself. There was this science challenge and he baked the solar system! Nearly destroyed the kitchen. But George is always good, so he couldn't, you know . . .'

'Turn around?' I suggest.

'Yes. And yesterday, he came back from school literally in tears, because the places went to two boys who are always rubbish, terrible behaviour, but who tried a bit harder in the last few weeks.'

I sympathize with this. I sympathize with Miss F too. George is so perfect. So blond and neat and clever and balanced and comes from such a supportive home – of course Miss F wanted to give the place where it was needed, to the children to whom it would mean a lot. Except it meant a lot to George too.

'And when he told his big sister,' continued Jeannie, 'Annie was just: welcome to my world. Get used to it, because that's how it is, in secondary too. And she told George, you know, it's because you've got everything already. But George just thinks it's because Miss doesn't like him.'

Ping! Miss T chimes in. *The trouble is*, she texts, *they think that because everyone knows that Phillip is best, he doesn't need the prize. But that's just why he has to have it. Because if they give it to someone else, they are actually positively taking it away from Phillip. They're saying, the teachers don't like you either. And we the teachers are also part of an anti-intellectual culture. This isn't acceptable, and I am going to stop it.*

And so, in Miss T's school, after everyone has enjoyed the always-epic spectacle of Miss T digging in her tiny sharp heels, the English prize goes to Phillip and not Tanya Turnaround. In Annie's school, the Maths prize goes to a boy the staff seem to like better than Annie, a smilier, more charming student, and in fact she never wins a Maths prize, not ever, not until she gets to Cambridge, the only student from her school in a decade, and starts getting top marks in the Pure papers. In our school, there are two Maths prizes: one for Achievement, which goes to my son and his nerdy ilk, and one for Progress, which goes to Tanya Turnaround. This is probably as decent a compromise as can be arranged, but it still causes injustice and resentments which will be remembered for years.

Because people do care about prizes, and children especially so. They accept their judgement, even if it is a strange, wildly outdated judgement – fastest one hundred yard dash, Cup for Character, Trophy for a Drop Kick – sometimes for their whole lives. In our school, I insisted on everyone entering the national poetry competitions for young people, over and over again, until we started winning, until poetry became our top sport. Something alchemical came from that – something similar to the thing that keeps Eton producing cabinet ministers. Which is why we can't abolish prizes, even if the harm done to the disappointed may well be larger than the good done to the winner. To misquote Frank O'Hara, 'these things do have meaning. They're strong as rocks.'

About Selection: Sets and Streams, Grammars and Not

Jez and Oldest One

Jez's Joke

We were having a speaking competition. The hall was filled with unfamiliar uniforms, and an earnest girl in a kilt was just stepping down from the podium after a long address about climate change, linked, as it so often is, to littering.

Then Jez and his team took the stage. They were from a country school with traditional blazers. Jez was busting out of his: a big lad with a strong wrist and heavy neck, an unbuttoned collar, a pushed-down kipper tie. He was further constrained by the conventions of the competition: the elderly, fussy format of the English-Speaking Union which requires one to have a chairman and voter of thanks, which encourages prissy jokes and empty praise.

But Jez seemed determined to bust out of these, too. He leant back on his elbows, scowling, as his (small, anxious) chairman introduced him: 'a popular character who goes over the top sometimes'. He waddled confidently forward and leaned over the lectern. 'My speech,' he said, 'is about Mixed Ability.' *Miss Debility*, he pronounced it, in his glottal, country accent, as if the concept were a particularly wearing teacher. 'Miss Debility. I'm against it.'

In front of me, the young teacher from the private school, whom we'd brought in to do the assessment, nodded sadly in agreement. He ticked his 'intro' boxes, ready to give Jez good marks. His school spent much time sub-dividing already highly selected pupils, until, like tiers of angels, the very cleverest spoke in their pure voices only to each other. Miss Debility in charge of a country comprehensive probably sounded horrifying to him.

I shared a grin with Miss T. We were hoping for some gossip about Jez's school; we'd heard they'd had Ofsted in, just last year. Miss T, I knew, was also suspicious of Mixed Ability. It messed up her marking schemes and militated against her pathological drive to push each child beyond their maximum.

To be honest, the term made me brace my shoulders, too. Mixed Ability – and Jez in fact, with his rough and ready country demeanour – called to mind my first school, crowded classrooms of Mixed Ability eleven-year-olds, and the extremely elaborate rookie lesson plans I'd made in an attempt to differentiate. We'd been to outer space once, I recalled, in a six-week-long writing project in which they all designed rockets and kept logs and I had to mark them all over half term and . . . well, that was before I had children. I didn't think I could do that, now.

But Jez wasn't a nice, keen Year 7 who wrote over-long logbooks about imagined galaxies. He was a rambunctious Year 9 in a mixed comprehensive which just this year, he told us, following that Ofsted visit, had switched from very strong setting in every subject, 1–4, to Miss Debility for everything. Jez didn't know why this had occurred, but he was very clear it was a disaster. Now nothing was happening in his lessons. He was bored, he said, gazing up at us with ferocity and sorrow, bored till he could eat himself, arm first.

At my elbow, Miss T murmured in sympathy. There was nothing she abhorred more than a bored, bright kid, because that was what she had been herself in a school not unlike Jez's. The audience – swotty children and their keen parents, mostly – nodded too. Probably, most of them saw themselves in some version of a top set, perhaps even a school-sized top set, a grammar. The Weald of Kent Grammar School was in the news just then, battling to open an 'extension' school, and it was easy to see the congruence of vision: a light, happy classroom, where ideas were freely exchanged, behaviour was perfect, and the children, even those as sturdy as Jez, could 'really fly', freed from the dead weight of their peers.

There were probably some 'dead weight' kids in the room too – ones with dyslexia, perhaps, or an inconvenient illness, or just nerves. But, showing true demagogic skill, Jez moved on before we could worry about them. The thing was, he said, it wasn't just him! He'd been talking to – and here his chairman eyed him meaningfully, clearly wondering what term he might blurt out – some of the less academic kids in his year, and the ones who were the thickest – dark look from the chairman – they hated Miss Debility worse than he did! The lessons were going far too fast for them! They couldn't keep up, and then they gave up! It was awful.

Vocabulary faux pas or not, the audience was still nodding, even Miss T. Again, the point was a solid one: students with real difficulties aren't usually loudest against sets, even if their own set is called 4. Kids with dyslexia, dyscalculia, ASD, or a whole range of general mild delays often have scalding experiences of mainstream classrooms and do much better in a small group moving at an easier pace, preferably with skilled teaching assistants. Set 4s in our school, certainly, were often surprisingly kindly places; there were several teachers who preferred and specialized in them.

But then Jez hit the sticky patch in his speech. He was now supposed, according to the marking criteria, to expand his case and improve his point with examples. Data. Case studies. Twined in personal anecdote maybe, but you needed them: facts. But Jez havered. The young assessor's hand moved down the marking sheet, and stopped, expectantly.

Undaunted, Jez announced a 'visual aid'. He'd done a survey of his class, 'Miss Debility, for and against', and his chairman was holding up a graph in marker pen of the result. The assessor put a question mark in the box.

Jez, it was sadly clear, hadn't read much educational theory. But then, it might not have mattered if he had. Setting and grammar schools is overwhelmingly an emotional issue. A few years on, in September 2016, Justine Greening, Secretary of State for Education, wouldn't be able to produce any strong data in support of grammar schools in parliament, and she had presumably been well briefed in educational research. Nor could the briefing paper on grammar schools produced for the House of Commons Library a few weeks later, because, however intuitively true it feels, creating Set 1, or isolating clever children, does not allow them to 'fly', or at least not sufficiently high to be statistically significant. At best, the briefing paper reckoned, the UK's 163 grammars – schools that suck in remarkable amounts of parental energy, which are among the most socially selective in the country, which choose less than 3 per cent of their intake from those on free school meals – allow their students to gain about a third of a grade extra in each GCSE relative to their starting point than an average school. Many comprehensives also achieve this sort of differential, and others – ours – achieve much more, and achieve it across the board, for the limited as well as the clever, for the poor as well as the rich.

Here in the debate hall, Jez's material was getting thinner and thinner. He had very little to say, and no figures, about the kids in his class who were probably most affected by setting: not the clever ones, in fact, and not the 'thick' ones either, not even the middling and willing Set 2 ones, but the middle-to-low-ability ones – Set 3. Probably, Jez had good reasons to forget them. They may well have made paper darts of his survey or mocked his ambition in taking part in a speaking competition. Probably, Jez didn't like them much.

Because no one likes Set 3, not even other pupils, and certainly not teachers. Set 3 are no fun. Many of them have behavioural problems and poor concentration – otherwise they'd be in Set 2. A few of them don't like your subject (and therefore you the teacher) in particular. A few more are in Set 2 elsewhere and let you know it. Some of them are just drearily mediocre. All of them know that the carrot you are dangling – a pass at GCSE, for instance – isn't in their reach, because that is the way the UK education system was designed in the fifties and how it still operates: sheep to go one way to university, goats to go to work. There is a shibboleth, a gate, to divide them, and here Set 3 get stuck. But, unlike Set 4, they are not humble enough to accept this judgement. They do not agree that they are goats. They will not consent to want carrots such as a good D and improved spelling; they want a good life and good prospects, just like Sets 1 and 2. The psychic wound of exclusion falls heaviest on Set 3, because they are bright enough to see that the system exists and that they are the losers in it, but not organized enough to do anything about it. Set 3 are angry.

So no one wants to teach Set 3, and, in weak schools, weak heads of department give in to the pressure and give Set 3 to the weakest teacher, or the temporary teacher, or the newly qualified one. In comprehensives, the problems of Set 3 are also often compounded by social class; into Set 2, disproportionately, are piled the middle-class kids whose decent attitude helped them through primary; into Set 3, disproportionately, are slid the working-class, surly but able kids whose manners and background did not help them at all. Even without across-the-board streaming, which is very rare these days, Set 3 often find themselves sitting next to each other in English, Maths, and Science, feeling helpless and angry; exhausting and enraging their teachers, destroying their best and most hopeful lessons, making sure they cannot be taught in any creative or relaxed way; having no fun. And so they feel more and more angry and multiply their own problems until one group of Set 3 Year 9 kids are disrupting an entire school.

And this, though he did not know it, was what had happened in Jez's school. Since the day it joined up its secondary modern and grammar buildings thirty years previously, it had streamed and setted ferociously, often echoing in the arrangement of its classes the social divisions of the market town around it. This, compounded in recent years by weak leadership and a high turnover of teachers (property prices in the town were terrifying), had resulted in a divided school where the top sets were shiny and everyone else ran feral: a school with a sort of internal grammar and secondary modern system. For a long time, though, the school still looked good on results day because the results were smoothed out into a decent average. Then government data started to reveal academic progress since primary rather than raw results, and the picture was not pretty. In this school, only the top sets learned as well as they should, and middle-ability children from disadvantaged backgrounds – Set 3 – did astonishingly badly; some learning less in five years of secondary education than in three of primary, some not moving forward at all, one or two actually going backwards.

Jez's school, in fact, was a neat example of the mathematical law of setting: that the good done to the selected minority is always smaller than the bad done to the rejected majority. There is a related mathematical law, the Formula of Grammars, which runs: because each grammar creates three secondary moderns, and because secondary moderns are giant, locked-down Set 3s – places where no one wants to teach because it is no fun; where achievement in the exam system is always just out of reach; where poor and badly behaved children are disproportionately piled; where problems breed and multiply – the good done by grammars is always less than the bad done by secondary moderns by a factor of at least three.

But setting and grammars are, as we've said, emotional issues, not maths. Certainly, they are for Theresa May, Justine Greening's boss. Her policy of expanding grammar schools, expounded from the time she came to power in 2016 until the election of 2017, seemed to be a passion project, because it flew in the face of all research, and opposition not just from Labour and the Lib Dems, but May's own party – in the face of everyone, in fact, except the *Daily Mail*.

But May went to a grammar school herself, one in a country town much like Jez's: Holton Park. So perhaps her mission is a consequence of an even older law than the Formula of Grammars, the rule that everyone wants to reproduce the school they went to, however much they hated it themselves. While Theresa May was at school, the establishment changed from a girls' grammar into the comprehensive it still is, Wheatley Park School. I once met a contemporary of May's and he said the transition, like the sudden de-setting of Jez's classes, was abrupt and terrible.

Imagine it: a large country village in the early seventies,

divided on class lines like Jez's, but probably even more bitterly. On one side of town, a girls' grammar headed by the vicar's daughter, with a delicate hierarchy of World War II schoolmistresses and fifties-style prim discipline; on the other, a secondary modern dedicated to turning out ploughmen and their wives. And one bad day, without much preparation or kindness, they are amalgamated. The result is chaos and bitterness and numerous unrecorded acts of cruelty: a disaster. And ever after – whatever the evidence to the contrary – the prim, inflexible, cross Head Girl believes in her gut that a comprehensive means letting the bad boys in to spoil everything, and when she becomes Prime Minister, she sets out to recreate the school of her dreams for good girls everywhere. The ones who have passed their exams, of course. The ones who deserve it.

Though to do so, she must face out Ofsted and their ilk, and Ofsted are on to the Formula of Grammars. They are watching progress now, not raw results, which was why, despite its very average overall performance, they had decided to inspect Jez's school the year before his speech, and why their recommendations were so bald: Mixed Ability, now. Jez, said the experts, would be OK, even if he did eat his own fist. Jez would find his own resources – look, he had just signed himself up for a speaking competition, and he had, definitely, you could tell from his teacher's aghast expression, written his own speech. Jez would pass his exams just fine, while his classmates would be freed from the shackles of inferiority, and flourish.

But Jez himself wasn't convinced. He hadn't finished his speech either. As a final morsel, he leaned meaningfully over the lectern. 'I'm just going to leave you wiv a liddle joke,' he said. 'Mixed Ability.' It took us a while to laugh.

'Poor old Jez,' said Miss T. 'Shall we tap him and get him to move to us? He could get the bus.' Because Miss H, finest and most liberal of all heads of English, insists on setting 1–4 from Year 7 on. And Miss T, who eats educational data for breakfast and has a long-time crush on Sir Michael Wilshaw, fully agrees with her; and so, probably, despite everything I have just said about Set 3, do I. We believe in setting the way we believe in democracy: the best worst system devised so far.

Really, it comes down to practicalities. School funding allows for about twenty-five pupils in a set. In our school, the range of ability in any year group runs from those who are reading *Jane Eyre* to those with not a word of English. Teaching this range within a single class means many small groupings and individual projects, which takes hours of teacher time. Therefore, we set 1–4, cramming the top sets with thirty-plus pupils and giving the space, smaller groups, and teaching assistants to the lower sets. All teachers, including Miss H, take a turn at all sets, including the dreaded Set 3. No one is locked in; student movement between sets is frequent. Miss H regularly faces down Ofsted surveys with her own data. We are overwhelmingly successful; each year all our students make outstanding progress, much better than a grammar, and those in Set 3 do especially well. Statistics, thinks Miss H, should be as detailed and local and small scale as possible. What works, works.

Though surely Miss H would baulk at Jez's marker pen

survey: she has standards. It cost Jez dear, too; the girl with the climate change speech took the cup. But funnily enough, three years later, Jez's figures turned out to be right. Despite Ofsted intervention, his cohort would record the worst GCSE results their school had ever seen, terrible across the board, and catastrophic especially for bright, disadvantaged students – Jez.

Ofsted came back in, and the report was direr than ever. Behaviour in the school had collapsed, just as Jez said, just as it did in Theresa May's school. The bitterness of the excluded had taken years to establish, and without strong leadership or real belief in what they were doing, it destroyed the school. Jez was right: there was only one place where he could flourish in the British class and classroom system, and that was at the bottom end of the top set of a securely run comprehensive, a place where he could hold on to his working-class identity while stretching his fine brains, where he could see other aspirations while holding his own. Miss Debility did take that away from him; the joke really was on him.

Oldest One's Not-Grammar School

Now Oldest One is sixteen and we've crossed town to check out the sixth form in the Famously Good Comp. It's huge (five hundred pupils). Its results at A Level are among the best in the country. They have STEP Maths and a brass quintet. It's tempting, much as we love our school. Oldest One's year group is very small, and the number going into the sixth form even smaller, so the courses on offer are limited. Here, they have A Level Music, two Further Maths sets, Economics, Theatre Studies, and three foreign languages. I can't imagine how they do it; the funding per pupil in the sixth form has been in decline since the Tories came to power.

We're nervous, so we're early. We tour the facilities, which are pleasingly minimal: battered classrooms and overcrowded bike racks; clearly, teaching gets priority here. I collect a prospectus, and study it. You are admitted to each A Level course separately . . . you must have a B at GCSE in your chosen subject . . . you need to have six Bs overall. It's well within Oldest One's range, but it would exclude most of the other pupils in Year 11 at his current school. And surely – this is a puzzle – quite a few in Year 11 in this school too, because it may be Famously Good but it is still a comp, and at least a third of them don't get their five GCSEs with English and Maths each year. What do they do for sixth form? And there's another, related mystery: I can't find re-sit GCSE Maths and English anywhere on the prospectus, but they must be there. They are basic, essential qualifications. Doesn't every state sixth form in the country offer them? In Essex, they were our bread and butter.

I keep leafing through, looking, as we stand around in the lobby. My son is watching kids in private school uniforms come in, lots of them, and snarling, sotto voce, for he is going through a purely Marxist phase. We check out the display stands: Oxbridge Entrance, Extra-Curricular . . . but wait, here is a stand from Local Rough Academy, the most disadvantaged school in the whole city, the one that, in addition to the poverty we carry in our school, educates most of the poor white, as opposed to immigrant kids. What can this be doing here?

'Are you looking for a BTEC in PE?' says a voice from behind the stand, and a chummy lady with optimistic cat's-eye glasses on a glittery chain manifests herself, smiling eagerly.

'Hruumph,' says Oldest One. He still hates being spoken to in public.

But the lady is not put off. Clearly underemployed at this stage in the evening, and also taking slouched and scruffy Oldest One for a disaffected youth, she spiels: 'A Levels aren't for everyone! The important thing is to find the course that is for you. We have a full range of BTECs. We have Business! Are you interested in Business?'

'No!' says Oldest One, who already has highly developed quasi-Marxist views about this subject.

'You can take it alongside re-sit English and Maths,' says the lady, kindly, and the penny drops.

'Oh wow,' I say, excited to have cracked it. 'You're here to mop up the Year 11 kids who are going to get chucked out of Famously Good Comp! They have to come to you because they can't do re-sit English and Maths here! That's what happens to the GCSE failures!'

'And then Famous Comp tops up with private school dropouts,' mutters Oldest One, Marxist-ly.

'The important thing is to find a course for the individual,' the lady says, blandly. 'We don't all have the same talents.'

'Do you do any A Levels at your place?' I ask.

'No,' she says.

'I see! So you're like the secondary modern sixth form?' I bulldoze on. 'And Famously Good Comp is the grammar, and you're working together?'

'We co-operate to maximize choice for the individual,' says the lady, firmly.

Honestly, I can see Famous Comp's problem. It's the curse of A Level, again: exams conceived for 10 per cent of the country and designed to be taught in groups of fifteen, now funded to be taught to 70 per cent of the population in groups of twenty. What is Famous Comp to do? To maintain its famous, wide-ranging, excellent sixth form it must have a wide choice of A Levels. To pay for that, including the minority small classes such as Music, the rest of the classes must be filled up to twenty. A full A Level class is stressful on teacher and students, and the demand of the course means even a moderately weak student in such a class will fail. Failing your A Level is no good to anybody, but offering alternative BTEC classes for weaker students alongside the A Level probably won't work, because they will be seen as second rate and will be very hard to fill. Besides, lots of BTECs demand facilities like kitchens and workshops.

So Famous Comp is making its A Level classes economic by stacking them high, but workable by packing them only with students who can cope. It is achieving this by excluding anyone, including pupils from its own lower school, who didn't pass English and Maths first time: a crude, but probably accurate enough measure. The others go to Rough Academy. Rough Academy, in turn, gives up its brightest students to Famous Comp to do A Levels, and compensates by filling up its BTEC classes to economic levels. Nice. The only problems, in fact, are the individual students hurt when their school excludes them for not being clever enough (this is a big hurt); the expectations and academic standards hurt all the way down Rough Academy by the lack of an academic sixth form; the difficulties caused in staff recruitment at Rough Academy because the best teachers will always want an academic range; and the underlying, pus-filled wound of social division which this system so clearly exasperates.

'Doesn't it break your heart?' I say to the lady from Rough Academy. 'When you work in the school. I mean, honestly, doesn't it?'

The lady puts down her leaflet. 'Kind of,' she says. 'Yes.'

Nevertheless, we tour the Famous Comp History Department, and talk to the empowered, informed, highly successful Oxbridge entrance officer. We chat to some of the kids crowding in: Oldest One's clever contemporaries who left the state system at different points for St Egg's, for rural comps, for private school, each time impoverishing his classrooms and his life, all flowing back now the Not-Grammar offer is on the table. And we are here, too. It's not the children's fault. When Oldest One gets over his Marxism he'll like them, very much.

So Oldest One goes to Famous Not-Grammar for his sixth form, taking his best mate with him, thus depriving his own old school, my dear school, of both their fine brains. But he flourishes in the big, fast-moving classes, and he likes his new, posher, intellectual friends. Though he comments that the standard of behaviour is lower, on the whole, in Famous Comp than in our place, and that middle-class kids 'definitely, definitely drink more and take way more drugs. The kid who takes the most, most drugs? He got expelled from a private school. It's really simple: the more money, the more drugs. People who think our school is rough? They know nothing.'

About Teaching English

Michael and Allen

When I started to teach English, I wondered if anyone else – in the school, in the district, in the country – was teaching the correct use of the apostrophe, for whichever year group I informed about it, it always seemed to be news. Perhaps all rookie English teachers have the same experience: standing in front of class after class and imparting the truth about the possessive to a row of round-eyed faces to whom it is entirely novel. I was flattered, filled with missionary zeal, and my earnest evangelizing lasted until I found myself explaining the apostrophe as a brand-new idea to the very same pupils whom I had so carefully enlightened the previous year. Thus, I discovered that all English teachers do teach the apostrophe; the problem is, the apostrophe doesn't stick.

Of course, all schooling is a broad brush, all lessons dripping paint. There will always be gaps and corners it is impossible to cover; that shouldn't stop us slopping on the whitewash. But the apostrophe seemed special; the rule was easy enough to teach, but peculiarly hard to retain.

I'd explain it, everyone would get it; then its and didnts, and, worse, acres of grocers' apostrophes (apple's and pear's), would appear in the very next essay. In fact, when I was teaching re-sit GCSE in Essex and my only aim was to get the kids to pass the exam, somehow and anyhow, I would tell my classes on no account to use the apostrophe, never, no, not at all, because I reckoned this created fewer mistakes than the reverse.

So why won't the rules about the apostrophe adhere to the mind when, for instance, the line 'screw your courage to the sticking-place' always does? They are both arcane and complex; both appeal to lost word forms. Perhaps *Macbeth* is simply more useful. We all find moments when we need to tighten our determination like a lute string, but no one actually needs the apostrophe to communicate other than the most delicate writers and elegant readers; for ordinary purposes we know what 'didnt' means, perfectly well, as a billion txts demonstrate. Most of the time, in fact, the apostrophe is used less to communicate than as a badge of education. Grocers misuse the apostrophe because they are worried about this; they know the concept of the apostrophe matters to some customers, so they add it to their pear's.

The grocers are right: people care. In fact, the large bag of stuff loosely called 'good grammar' and its prominent markers – the distinction between practice and practise, the proper use of the semi-colon and apostrophe, the decay of certain words – often seem to be the only aspect of English teaching that concerns governments, newspaper leader writers, and men on Clapham omnibuses at all.

There was a dramatic example of this in 2016, when eleven-year-olds across England were suddenly, by government edict, forced to do enormous amounts of grammatical parsing in their end of primary school exams. This exam was imposed against the advice of almost all teachers, writers, and educational researchers, but the Tory government insisted that it would raise standards; that for the baffled herds of reading, writing, shouting children, only grammar would do; only parsing could sort the sheep from the goats. The main result was that thousands of children were made very unhappy, failed the exam, and were put off English at secondary school.

I am not going to argue here that grammar does not matter, because that is rehearsed elsewhere, and besides, it matters very much to me. I treasure the apostrophe. I feel about the decay of certain words – 'disinterest', or 'literally', or 'unique' – as I do about elderly relatives in their final illness: a mixture of sorrow, rage, and denial. I have the greatest difficulty in saying 'relatable', though I push myself. But over the years I've learned that the best way to teach the apostrophe is by teaching the user to care about it and about all written expression; to teach reading and writing with confidence and love. These are some of the kids who taught me that.

The Ineffable Genius of Michael Egbe

To begin with, a poem, a whole poem, because that is the way I always begin a lesson. I don't apologize for this in a classroom, even if – especially if – the poem is complex or ancient, and I don't apologize now. This is an exciting piece of writing, the best thing you'll hear all week, I say. Also: brace yourselves; this is going to be wild. Though now I add: bear in mind that this poem was written by a seventeen-year-old from Nigeria, a boy, who like so many others, was left behind with an aunt when his parents first came to England to work in the NHS, and who only joined his family when he was fourteen; a boy who did a lot of dreaming and a lot of longing, and who had to grow up very quickly. Buckle up and feel his velocity.

Cape
By Michael Egbe

When I was a kid, I was always waiting for that
    freak accident,
the one that would cause the awesome explosion, that
would spread gamma rays down my blood stream; for
    that
rush, that rage, as my cells fused with this strange
    element.

I could see myself on a hospital bed surrounded
by doctors unable to explain the marvel I am.
I knew I would feel no pain as a needle tried
to pierce my skin, impenetrable as a turtle's shell,

and that soon I'd wake up and see my flabs
turn to abs, my biceps bulge out of my sleeves

and I'd try to walk but end up defying gravity and
– quickly forgetting how terrified of heights I am –

slip into that skin-tight costume with the silky cape
that moves and rustles with the wind
as I stand at the top of the Empire State Building
glaring into the clear blue sky, and

(momentarily ignoring the beautiful brunette reporter
who was going to fall deeply in love with me
when I revealed my mysterious secret identity to her
and asked her to be my bride)

swoop down to the street to that small fat kid
who'd just been dipped in the toilet by his high
    school bullies
and give him courage to fight back not with violence
but with the aim to change them for the better, and

fly him around in my cape and tell him that I've got
    him.

When Michael first wrote that poem, and I found myself
typing it out and correcting only the spellings (quite a
few of these – to be fair, I think Michael may be a little
dyslexic, like so many of my poets), it seemed so good
that I worried I might be losing my mind and sense of
perspective, becoming my fear: the poetic equivalent of a
crazy cat lady who thinks each puss is a genius. So I sent
it to Professor K, up at the university, to check; then read

it again, putting in, mostly for fun, the brackets and the final stanza break.

But that was all I could add to it. Everything else was perfect. It really didn't seem possible or natural. The poem had been written, entirely in front of me, in less than an hour. Michael had chatted for at least twenty minutes of that; giggled to himself through most of the composition process; and added that brilliant title, with something like a smirk, only at the very last minute. It was even stranger because, though Michael was a talented musician and could tango, he was not, officially, clever. He was always losing things. He scraped a B at English GCSE. He got an ignominious U when he attempted the AS in English Language. But this poem, this poem was –

Ping! *So moving. So sophisticated,* came the Professor's assessment. *So much to say about contemporary masculinity. The yearning! The way he rescues himself at the end! And then the sounds scheme, those full rhymes only for the cartoon self. And the tone – he's sort of playing with us throughout. Swooping – like Superman. Yup, this really does it for me. How did you get him to write that?*

How did I? Well, there was a trick to it, but a very simple one. I'd started the workshop by handing out the poem below, which is by Lorraine Mariner. (Lorraine Mariner is one of my favourite poets for many reasons, but one of them is that she comes from Essex, and went to one of my sixth-form college's feeder schools just before the college itself came into being. Her deadpan, loving, hilarious accounts of Essex life, and her powerful vein of self-deprecating, ironized fantasy, remind me of Liam.) It's

a rich poem, and particularly appealing to teenagers just
emerging out of childhood, and rueing, as they always do,
the loss.

My Beast

When I was a child I worried
that when I got my chance to love a beast
I would not be up to the task and I'd fail.

As he came in for the kiss I'd turn away
or gag on the mane in my mouth
and the fair-haired prince
and the dress that Beauty wore
on the last page of my Ladybird book
would be lost to me forever.

But now I see that the last thing my father
driving home late from work
would have on his mind is the gardens
flashing past and he would never stop
to pick a rose for one of his daughters
and if some misfortune such as

his Volvo reversing into a beast's carriage
did occur and I ended up at the castle
as compensation, the beast would probably
just set me to work cleaning and I'd never
look up from scrubbing a floor and catch him
in the doorway admiring my technique.

Still, as I've heard my dad say,
he and his children may not always
be brilliant but they always turn up,
and in time when the beast comes to realise
that I haven't tried to escape
he'll give me leave one Sunday a month

to visit my family and access
to his vast library and in bed at night
reading by the light of a candle
I'll shut another calf-bound volume
and hear its quality thud
with something like happiness.

And you can see that Michael's poem is like Mariner's in
some ways: they both have that ironic tone Professor K
admired so much, and the overlong, tense sentences,
bounding from stanza to stanza; they both appear to have
regular stanzas and iambic lines and in fact burst out of
them; they are both about childhood stories and fantasies;
they both have unexpected, moving endings and marvellous, deadpan titles.

But Michael's poem is in no sense a copy; if anything,
it's a reading of the source poem, because it takes on the
gender question raised by her poem so cleverly and powerfully. Mariner's is about female stereotypes and fantasy,
about Beauty and the Beast, that powerful ancient tale
of being sold to a hideous husband and learning to love
enslavement, a story she subverts first with the image of
her real, kindly father in his Volvo, and then with the

'calf-bound volume' with its 'quality thud' which symbol-
izes freedom of the mind. Michael's poem replies with an
equally powerful account of a masculine stereotype – the
Superman story, the cape of power – and subverts that
by showing the whole Superman story to be a fantasy of
rescue. The boy with his head in the toilet is clearly the
same child who is waiting for the 'freak accident'; they
both need to be wrapped in a cape and reassured. And
then there is the aspect of display and dress-up: the flut-
tering cape that is put on to be seen, just as, more
conventionally, a woman puts on a dress. I could not have
hoped for a more powerful or accomplished literary reply,
in short, if I'd lectured my MA students for an hour and
set the task as coursework.

But no lecturing had happened at all. No one mentioned
iambs, or stereotypes, or subversion, or even gender. All
we did, in our group of teenagers sitting round in the
library – all I ever do, in fact – was read the poem, and
chat, not about how the poem worked, but about what it
provoked in us. We talked about Disney's princesses and
Superman a lot, because we were a very multicultural
group, and these were our universal gods, and then we
drifted on to what we planned to ask for when the fairy
finally appeared and offered us three wishes; and about
time-turners, and self-renewing purses, and wings, which
of course everyone had hoped to have.

I shushed them and read the poem aloud again while
they sat with their eyes shut. Then I asked them to begin
writing with the phrase: 'When I was a child,' and to write
down a childhood dream which makes them blush, now,

actually makes their skin prickle. And after a long time of pens scratching, I gave them another prompt: to put a turn in their poem, a different perspective: 'but now I see.' And that was it.

So all the cleverness of Michael's poem – its varied rhythm and sound, its delicate play of tone, irony, and expectations – came from what he had absorbed from the Mariner poem, just from listening to it, not analysing it. If we had spent time on discussing literary features, in fact, it is highly likely that Michael would have lost interest, because, though Michael clearly has what poets call a golden ear, his metalanguage – his vocabulary for discussing language – is particularly weak. When I showed him Prof K's analysis of the sounds of his poem, he was pleased, but baffled. He really didn't know what the Professor meant.

This paradoxical mismatch of talents – the pronounced ability to pick up and reproduce poetic shapes and sounds solely by listening to them, teamed with an equally marked inability to analyse writing – is not uncommon; Michael is merely an extreme example. Only a couple of the students in the room during the Mariner workshop could have written a decent A Level-style analysis of her poem, yet all of them wrote interesting versions of the poem, picking up different elements of the tone, theme, and sound. For example, this is Helen's, who was twelve at the time, and, as you can tell, bookish and brilliant.

I wanted to be
the girl with the twelve-mattressed four-posted bed.

Not a princess, just an ordinary girl
who never felt the pea.

I wanted to be
the woman in a meadow of brown grass and flowers,
wanted my hair to curl in a spiral
and blow in the wind.

I wanted to be
Amy March with her pickled limes,
wanted to stand a proud
pretty crosspatch in front of the class.

I wanted to be
a hidden face in the snowy picture book,
wanted to watch the snake in the casket
from the frosted hedge,

wanted to see it bite the children,
wanted to be indifferent.

Yet even someone as clever as Helen disappears into a
creative haze of A4 and orange gel pen when she writes,
and if you were to nudge her mid-way, and ask her to point
to a metaphor, or just an inspirational line from the source
poem, she would not be able to do so.

But then, neither could I. When I'm in the middle of
writing a poem, or any piece of writing, even this, I also
feel as if I am in a fog of sound and images, feel that I am
building a bridge, stick by stick, in the direction of what I

hope, but could not swear, is the other side of the river. It's an absorbing, crafting, instinctive process which feels entirely different from the critiquing/labelling/essay-writing one I have so painfully learned over many years. I'm prepared to bet, in fact, that critiquing happens in a different part of the brain, and that only the editing and drafting process of writing, especially the final polishing stages, use both areas.

While Michael and Helen were absorbed in writing their poems, they leant on the Mariner poem; in particular, they both borrowed that shapely shift in perspective from adult to child which is the keystone of all three poems. So they were responding to the poem, but not critiquing it. This is not a student or beginner's writing process. I'm always echoing or answering or leaning on another poem when I write, too; it's just that because I have read so much verse, it usually isn't clear to me which piece I have in mind. For example, I once wrote a poem about Simeon Stylites without consciously remembering that I had read, and even written an essay about, a Tennyson poem on the same subject a decade previously. When I finally came to look up Tennyson's poem – long after my own poem was published – I found I had begun mine with the same word: 'Although'.

All poets lean and borrow and echo. Poems come from poems; part of the game of literary criticism is to trace the ways they build on, love, hate, knock down, answer, abuse, and adore each other. But that game ignores something much simpler: the universal, the gloriously ordinary, the simply human capacity to answer a speech pattern with a speech pattern, a poem with a poem. It's like responding to a dance step with a dance step, or singing a note back to a note: it's a thing we can all do; though, as with dance and singing, some individuals are much more deft, elegant, and interested than others, and a few, like Michael and Helen, have a notable gift. If you doubt me – try it. Without thinking too hard, write down a few lines beginning: 'When I was a child, I worried,' then listen to what you have done. You'll echo that iambic beat too, that deadpan tone. But you'll write your own poem.

In school, I rarely have more than an hour a week with any group, so I've come to lean on this echoing capacity almost to the exclusion of everything else. The quickest way I know to get results, and to let everyone write something good, is to give the students a great poem, and, without letting too much anxiety and analysis get in the way, give them the space to sing me one back. The poem chosen is very important; it needs to sound beautiful and to be emotionally direct – like the Mariner one.

Poems don't produce copies of themselves; they accommodate and differentiate. Beginners will cling to the frame of a poem, the rhetoric or repetitions. Experienced poets are much more independent. They will riff off a line or two, pick up a rhythm, a title, and – always my final instruction – lose my prompts entirely. Everyone gets to read at least one rich poem in my workshops, but the most talented students start to read a lot of poetry for themselves, and to read like poets: observing, stealing, and storing. Similarly, I edit and type up the work of the beginners, bringing out the best in them, but the better students start to edit and re-draft their own poems more and more intensely, learning to visit them from a more critical, outside perspective. Usually – though not Michael Egbe – they finish by acquiring a metalanguage (metaphor, simile, iamb, metre, stanza, line break) to enable them to talk to themselves and others about what they are doing.

Learning to write like this is like mastering a musical instrument: first you learn to make a good noise through imitation and playing along with other people; then you learn to study your own and others' technique; finally, and as an option or addition, you write critically about your own and other people's music. Art is often taught like this too: tracing the lines of a photograph gives the bones of a picture; copying a great picture, brushstroke for brushstroke, is a well-established way of acquiring technique and understanding a painter's vision.

But playing an instrument and musical composition have always been a central part of the Music curriculum in this country, both at school and at university; and the practice of Art has always been the main component of its study. Writing poetry and fiction, though, is not part of the English curriculum, and in school, especially since the demise of the ill-starred and short-lived A Level in Creative Writing, there is no way of rewarding or marking what Michael and Helen have achieved. In English, we assess and value only that last part of the learning process: the metalanguage and the critical essay.

The reasons for this are complicated. English as an academic subject is much younger than Music, and when it was invented, at the end of the nineteenth century, there was a drive to make it taxing, analytical, and as much like Latin as possible, so that it could be respectable and taken seriously. Therefore, English composition, so babyishly easier and more pleasurable than Latin composition, was excluded. Creative Writing has since been re-introduced into universities, but via the US Liberal Arts model. This practice in turn is divorced from the study of literature; and its central teaching mode is the critical workshop when ambitious young writers photocopy their effusions and share them, which, notoriously, breeds sameness and personal paranoia. Wherever university Creative Writing teachers gather, they mourn that their students do not read, yet they never set an imitation as an exercise. Creative reading and creative response, which Michael, like so many students, finds so natural and so easy, and in which he demonstrates such talent, is not taught, or examined, in any university.

In schools, some creative response is allowed up to GCSE, but after the age of sixteen, English means A Level Literature or Language, and only a couple of syllabuses allow for even the smallest amount of creative response – or any kind of creative writing – to be shoehorned in by dedicated teachers. This focus on only one tiny area of English – critical response – has many toxic effects in schools, but one is to cut down the percentage of pupils continuing with English after the age of sixteen to less than 15 per cent. This is a tragedy: very, very few people – probably 15 per cent of that 15 per cent taking A Level – really enjoy the practice of criticism, but almost everyone enjoys writing and reading. Yet we have no 'Further English' in England;

no structure or reward for kids who don't want to write a 2,000-word essay on *Jane Eyre* but would like to write a story, who don't want to dissect a Shakespeare play but would like to read and see one, who would like to write a better letter, read another novel, who would like to read and write some poems. Who are entitled to read and write some poems.

Even in the younger years in school, the practice of creative writing and creative reading is under attack; there is certainly a great deal less of it, and less confidently taught, than when I began in teaching thirty years ago. But the decades since I did my PGCE have also seen the inexorable rise of the thing called 'formative assessment', and its lumpen classroom symptom, the WALT.

WALT is the acronym, as every schoolchild knows and every parent is surprised to learn, for We Are Learning To. WALTs are put on the board. They head the teacher's lesson plan. They are ruthlessly monitored during teacher training. WALTs, the theory goes, interact with the curriculum meaningfully and let everyone know where they are. They break up the lesson into simple objectives that the children themselves understand.

WALTs are created for the best reasons: it's about empowering students to control their own learning and chart their own progress; it's about openness and democracy; it's about spreading out skillsets so everyone can find their tool; it's about opening what educationalists Black and Wiliam, in a highly influential essay read by every teaching student, called the 'black box', the hidden learning process. Tease out the strands of this process, goes the argument, think out exactly what the student is learning, then deliver that analysis back to them precisely, telling them what they have achieved, and what they can build on. This is 'formative assessment', because it forms and changes the student as well as marking him.

All of which sounds fine, sounds good, sounds liberal; except when you remember that Black and Wiliam were writing about the learning of engineering; except when you start wondering: what is the WALT for the lesson that led to Michael's poem? Should we say Michael is learning to read today, or to write? Shall we say he is learning to use irony, or to control half-rhyme, or to discuss gender issues or the use of clichés, or perhaps punctuation across stanza breaks? And even if you had spent a strenuous half-hour predicting the sort of things Michael might get from the lesson, and synthesizing them into a millefeuille WALT, a poem in itself – how would that have fitted Helen's very different reading and writing experience?

And then – how shall we assess what they have done? What Learning Objectives (LOs) has Michael met and how can he improve next time? What about Helen? Who has done better at learning about gender? Shall we ask Michael to try some repetition in his next poem? Or encourage Helen to move on with half-rhyme? Do any of these questions have any relevance at all to Helen or Michael as writers or as people? Does this 'formative assessment' form anything?

This is not a farce: these are real and serious questions. In the twenty-five years since I started teaching, teachers have been increasingly bullied and harassed over these sorts of classroom minutiae to the point where they genuinely feel that Ofsted will descend if they teach an unconventional, non-WALT lesson. This is bad for all teachers but is particularly so in subjects where learning compartmentalizes less tidily; it is harder to say what is going in your English lesson than your Maths lesson, in History than in Chemistry. For the creative parts of the curriculum, the pressure is cruel. When my colleague Linda revealed at a conference that she had taught her GCSE students poetry by writing creatively all the way up to GCSE, the listening teachers were genuinely frightened. They assumed her students were being deprived of 'skills' and would fail their exams. They were only comforted, and amazed, when Linda showed them that oddly enough, this had worked; her students all made outstanding progress, and especially in poetry. When I led, in 2016, a poetry teaching workshop for newly qualified teachers and started as I have here, with Michael Egbe, one young woman simply wept. She said, through her tears, that she was upset because she thought I was making fun of her. She had wanted to go into teaching to teach creative writing, but it didn't fit in the curriculum; it was impossible, she could not find the LO for it. You can't assess it. There isn't a WALT. The young teachers around her agreed. Creative writing is impossible because you can't break it up. It's too hard to strand, mark, and turn into data.

And yes, it is difficult to strand Michael's poem, because it is a good, tightly woven unit of language: a work of art. So is Lorraine Mariner's poem. And the process by which Michael turned one into the other is certainly too complex to describe; it is both great and ineffable. No WALT can compass Art or Greatness, for its own language is too crude. Formative assessment does not allow for ineffable processes, but this does not mean they do not exist, or that when Michael wrote 'Cape', learning was not happening. The black box of creation stays closed to the poet as much as to the reader; any poet will tell you that. This is not a teacher conspiracy, or snobbery; it is the way writing is. Nor is it a concealment. Writing is not a hidden process; it is merely a mysterious one. And it is mysterious only because it is complex; because it encompasses not just many processes of the mind, but those processes interacting with the collective mind, with literature and poetry.

So, no, it does not unpack easily. But there is no need to unpack a box when it is so well filled with the black stuff called, in Spanish, *duende*: the best thing to do with such a box and such blackness is to admire it and perhaps copy it. Michael didn't need formative assessment in the shape of a net of words to help him write the next poem. The poem itself was the words; the poem itself was formative. Summative assessment – *that was brilliant, Michael; you went well beyond yourself, Michael; we really love that poem, Michael* – is what is called for here, and then perhaps another poem, to form his writing further.

But even the best, most risk-taking teachers, such as Linda and my other school colleagues, will have trouble fitting another poem into the school curriculum. The formative assessment movement has pushed the curriculum towards ever more strands and categories of writing, and towards 'skills' which have to be acquired and ticked off lists: not just 'prose', but 'non-fictional prose', 'transactional prose', 'business prose'. Then, because good writing is in practice very similar across genres, and because rich writing is hard to strand, teachers are pushed towards extreme and thin examples of each of these genres. This is how the English lesson becomes the History lesson, a soggy one, and thousands of Year 7s across the country have sat down this year not with poems but with Wikipedia entries and ship maps, to commence a 'non-fictional writing unit on the *Titanic*', after which they have been deemed to gain certain 'non-fictional writing skills', ticked off a long and complicated list. Though generally, they haven't, for as surely as the rich text of a poem breeds another rich text, the thin text of the Wiki entry breeds a thin one. And that is how, too, the prospect of reading a poem to kids and letting them write one in response has become a dangerous activity, one to make an idealistic young English teacher weep with fear.

In my dreams, I write a giant, all-purpose WALT for the English corridor. The banner reads: *We are learning to write by reading and to read by writing.* I have the words embroidered on yards of silk, and artfully pinned from Miss H's classroom to Miss P's like bunting, arching prettily over the loos in the middle.

In my dreams, I inscribe above all the white boards, in fine italic, on brass, an answer to the second WALT question, which is 'How Will We Know When We've Learned It?': *We will know we are learning to read well when we recognize beauty and truth in our own writing and in others' writing. We will know we are progressing in writing at those times when we go beyond ourselves; when we express what we did not even know we meant in a graceful synthesis of words and sounds that is both ours alone and part of the richness of our languages and literatures. We will know we have learned much in English at various points in the future, near and far, when we express ourselves confidently in writing, and when we find joy and humour and wisdom in reading.* Amen.

In my dreams, we never need to write another WALT. In my dreams, my colleagues are trusted to choose great, rich texts to teach, and we all trust the texts to teach the children. We assess both creative and critical responses to them as their final exams. In my dreams, all kids write poems, and no one is afraid to say this is good or that their poems are good.

And as for Michael Egbe: Mr D taught him piano, Miss A taught him drama, and now he's at Liverpool Hope. He never did learn literary analysis, but he did start setting his poems to music. And I always thought that 'Cape', as it couldn't help Michael get an A Level, and never won a prize, should at least reach a few more people, and now it has.

Allen's Smithy

Once upon a time, in England, there existed a respected English course which trusted the teacher to set the texts, which could include creative response, which could be taken by students older than sixteen who didn't want to do A Level, and which had no exam at the end of it. It was

GCSE English Literature, Northern Board; it was available between 1987 and 1998; and it was assessed on a portfolio of coursework. I taught it in Essex, and much preferred it to the A Level that turned so many of my nice, keen, not very academic students into demotivated failures. On the GCSE you could set Essex-friendly texts and take time over them. Very weak kids could progress, and there was any amount of room at the top. In fact, the only problem with this glorious qualification was that most of the sixth-formers who wanted to study English had already passed GCSE, so uptake was low, and mainly consisted of wobbly students also re-taking English Language GCSE, and desperate for support.

Allen, though, had already passed a decent set of GCSEs and was in his second year of Science A Levels. There was nothing wobbly about him, either: a big, capable-looking lad who seemed already too old for school. In fact, with his loping gait and square shoulders and long-sighted gaze, he seemed not particularly suited to inside spaces, either – as if he'd be more comfortable on a hillside, perhaps with a gun dog. His manner was gentle, though, his deep voice carefully quiet, and his intent clear: he was taking this course because he liked literature and meant to get the best from it. Twice a week, he tucked himself manfully behind the desk, outsize shoulders at one end, boots out the other, picked up his books with hands the size of dinner plates, and gave them that distant, appraising stare, as if assessing them for conversion into something else, possibly a table.

I soon learned that he held books at a distance because

they spoke so loudly to him. He liked novels, loved plays, and was physically affected by poetry; an image made him flush to his eyebrows, a new idea sent him shuddering back in his seat, feet akimbo. And he wasn't just open to discussing the sorts of subjects that sparked paranoid silence in most of Essex kids – sexuality, racial identity, love, religion, emotions of all kinds – he was eager to talk about them, leaning over the desk, gesturing with those blacksmith's hands, long hazel eyes alight with interest. I never met his mother, but I thought he must have a nice one; how else do you learn to be so unafraid of your own, or other people's feelings?

To have so splendidly masculine a person fully engaged in the feminine project of reading was a huge gift in Essex. The class fell in behind him, and we read all sorts of things, that year, well beyond the syllabus, just because we could: Shakespeare, ee cummings, Lorca, Blake. Ah, Blake. Allen loved Blake. Once, he told me, he started reciting 'The Tyger' in Hollywood's, the largest of all the nightclubs, and his best friend disowned him. But 'The Tyger' was his favourite. For his final essay, he wrote, wrestling with the text as if it were wrought iron, six full pages solely on that.

'What do you reckon it means,' I asked him, mid-process, '"When the stars threw down their spears, / And watered heaven with their tears"?' I genuinely wanted to know. I haven't been able to figure it out, myself, I explained to him, that couplet. Is heaven a sort of goldfish bowl around the earth, which the stars are weeping into/on? And if it is, where have the spears gone?

'No,' said Allen, surprised at me. 'Don't you get it?

Honestly? The tears and the spears are the same thing. They're molten metal, hitting water. Heaven is like, the meniscus.' Which is a glorious, if deeply eccentric response, a glowing snow globe of vision definitely not allowable at A Level.

I kept Allen's portfolio (he got an A) in the back of my filing cabinet for twenty-five years, because it was so beautiful in itself, and because it represented me at the very top of my teacherly game too; I had taught him, and that class, as much as I possibly could. When, for the purposes of this book, I pulled it out to see if it was true that it was a brilliant and moving document – it was – and that a quarter of a century previously I really had been allowed to teach so much more freely than I am now – also true – I noticed his distinctive surname and looked him up on Google. The boy with the visions of Blake, it quickly transpired, hadn't gone to university. He'd gone directly from school as an apprentice into a modern smithy: a precision-engineering firm making parts for the aerospace industry. Twenty-five years later, he owned it and had hugely extended it. Now, he employed fifty people, making him the only managing director and self-made millionaire I've ever knowingly read ee cummings with.

And such a useful one, too! I gazed proudly at the LinkedIn page. Not a hedge-fund manager, not an estate agent, but a manufacturer of actual objects, one of the last in England, and in charge of a factory which trained its employees carefully and held on to them for a long time. The Tory Party's ideal human. Ha, I thought, chew on that, Michael Gove!

Unless, of course, poetry was nothing to do with it. Perhaps Allen didn't remember William Blake at all, just the skills gained in the class. Perhaps he did not remember me, either, because even though he had spent two hours a week for a year sharing his imaginative visions of poetry with me, which is a very intimate thing to do, we had also had a very decorous, respectful teacher–pupil relationship. I couldn't recall a single piece of personal information we'd ever shared.

It took me a year to message him on LinkedIn, and ask. His response was immediate, passionate, and nothing about skills: of course he remembered me. 'When we read books with you the world opened up,' he wrote. 'Your lessons were where I learned who I was, became conscious of myself, grew up. That time was so important to me, a free space.'

An emotional education: that is something else English teachers have always delivered. English: the lesson where you laugh about sex, and argue about war, and talk about jealousy. English: where you grow up. Growing up does not WALT well, any more than creativity does, and in the last decade, English teachers do. Growing up does not WALT well, but, like creativity, it happens when you read. When I looked back through Allen's folder again, I could see it happening to him. We'd read Farrukh Dhondy, Willy Russell, Jeanette Winterson before we settled on the poetry fiesta, and Allen had taken each text, crammed with its rich, subversive information, seriously and gently into his big hands and large mind. They had not made him into a poet or a writer, but the thoughtful, liberal man at the end of the portfolio had a wider emotional experience than the sweet boy at the beginning of it, as well as better information and a few more writing skills. Allen had taught me something too, about humility, and not looking at foot-balling, laddish, working-class boys with a dismissive eye. Some of them recite Blake in nightclubs.

It is tempting, here, to reduce this to function, too, and say that Allen's improved empathy made him a better manager of people. Allen himself takes a wider view. 'Your classroom was a space for my imagination to roam freely, with you just whistling me in when I needed it,' he wrote, confirming that there was indeed a hillside inside his head, and also that English is an ineffably useful subject, and should be available, preferably in the free, flexible way I was able to teach it to Allen, to everyone. And next time I address a gathering of anxious young English teachers I will be able to say that, and that everyone is entitled to poetry, and that reading it makes you grow up, emotionally and intellectually; the managing director says so.

About Being Out
of Place

Sofia, Janie, and Chris

Sofia's Spelling

Sofia is writing in the library, tucked in the quiet corner
that is ours on a Tuesday. Sofia is fourteen, but she looks
younger. She has a soft round face, soft curly hair, and big
glasses over wide, guileless, green eyes. The hand moving
across the paper is plump, and the writing it leaves behind
is noticeably childlike, full of pot hooks and strange cap-
itals. The spelling, if you look closely, is childlike too, with
homophones confused and random extra vowels. But this
is what the words say:

When Death comes
(After Mary Oliver)

and lifts
its tarred head like a crow.
When it kisses my cheek like
an aunt, mild
as a childhood disease,

when Death comes and haunts
the tree outside
and strokes my window
like a lover,

when it comes like
an office meeting, a presentation,
a side door
that you never noticed,
opening –

'Golly,' I say, as I read it, slowly, partly because of the spelling, partly because this is strong and surprising stuff, even for Sofia. 'Did you think of that just now?'

'No,' says Sofia. 'I had that idea in the week. I stored it in my head, you know? I hoped it would come out in Poetry. Oh, I've just thought of something.' And she resumes writing.

Sofia is one of my top poets. She's won three national awards in the last year. She is also dyslexic. So dyslexic that she could not read independently till she was ten; that she has a full statement of special needs, special computer programmes, extra lessons, an individual timetable; so dyslexic that much of school has been a torture to her, and so, even though she loves words and stories, is the library.

And please don't tell me that books
are a trapdoor to another world
because that door
never opened for me.

As she wrote last year.

When I trained to be a teacher, I was taught nothing formal about dyslexia; it came under Special Educational Needs (SEN), which I was not doing. As I went into classrooms, I had a bit of in service training that told me that children who couldn't spell, but seemed otherwise bright, and who reversed letters, such as 'b' and 'd', might be dyslexic, and should be referred to SEN. Later, there was an enthusiasm for yellow films laid over text, and yellow glasses, to help dyslexic students read, and more students were given extra time in exams. In my sixth-form college, I scribed for a couple in exams, and marvelled at the disjunction between their previous grades and the fluent paragraphs coming out of their mouths. Gradually, as I learned more, and the world learned more, I started to think of dyslexia as very widespread and very wide, a constellation of features which started with:

Difficulty with spelling
Slow reading
Clumsiness
Bad handwriting
Constantly lost
Terrible maths
Can't read the time.

Then widened to include some associated syndromes:

Dyspraxia: clumsy movement, difficulty with catching and gripping

Dyscalculia: difficulty with reading numbers
Dysgraphia: difficulty with handwriting
Something unusual about the way the right and left
hemispheres of the brain connect
An inherited condition – runs in families.

And then expanded again to include some more subtle
symptoms, such as:

Very competent reading and writing combined with
the inability to read one's own writing back
Usually competent spelling accompanied by wildly
inaccurate rendering of longer words, especially those
with multiple vowels, as if the words had been
learned by outline only
Rapid reading combined with the difficulties above
Inability to do a crossword or play Scrabble – as if
letters could not be a system, as if words could never
be detached from meaning
Terrible mental arithmetic scores combined with a
talent for algebra
Tendency to become overwhelmed if required to
remember more than one task at a time.

And then:

A lifetime of anxiety attacks about handwriting,
reading aloud, finding a direction, reading a map, the
clock, and a calendar.

And finally:

> Ability to visualize 3D space – for example, to pack
> the boot of a car, see where a large wardrobe would
> fit in a room, or lay out a poem
> To play chess and draughts
> To be an architect; disproportionately, they are dyslexic
> To sculpt, to scrimshander a carrot, to make a flower
> from a radish, a statuette from corrugated cardboard
> To join up ideas and images, to see one thing on top
> of another
> To draw
> Enhanced ability to listen to words, especially sounds
> And to make a poetic image
> And perhaps to be a poet.

To be dyslexic, says my friend Sally Davis, who teaches a
famous workshop about the experience, is to have a mind
like an old-fashioned champagne coupe: a very wide cup
of perception supported by a narrow, fragile pipe of
processing capacity.

Sometimes, a dyslexic person may become overwhelmed
by how much she takes in: for example, looking at a page of
writing when the white spaces shout as loudly to her as the
black letters; reading a map when every mark seems equally
important. She can't force all those perceptions down the
processing capacity; stuff gets jammed. In compensation, on
the way down, thing often adheres to thing in unusual ways,
making witchy intuitions, surreal truths, and poetic images.

I have a mind like that: a champagne coupe of perception, a narrow stem of processing. I don't know when I
noticed this, exactly – when I started to identify features
of the dyslexic spectrum as belonging to me, or to say:
'I'm a bit dyslexic, too' when I met dyslexic children – but
I think when I was about thirty-five. I would say now
that while I certainly never went through Sofia's pain,
most dyslexic features here are also mine. I have a
powerful visual memory that allowed me to 'photograph'
words as a child and so appear to learn to read well. But
I can only spell with a spell checker; can only make my
way around a town with satnav or iPhone; only know
right from left if I pretend, briefly, to hold a pen; can only
write down a phone number left on an answering machine
if I replay the message nine times, one for each number;
have never dared learn to drive because all roads are a
fog to me; only started to write when word-processing
was invented; would never have finished a book without
it. As for when I started to excuse myself some of my
chronic anxiety about these difficulties, or when I learned
to start avoiding the sorts of circumstances which cause
it: I haven't, yet.

But I am working on the positives. When I met Sofia,
I was able to say: 'If you're dyslexic, you may well be a
poet too.' And to tell her that most of the poets I knew
had no sense of direction and were chronically muddled;
that only one or two of them could drive; that they were
disproportionately left-handed; that Benjamin Zephaniah
was nearly as dyslexic as she was and wrote about it. And

now, whatever tortures she endures, she has, as she says, her diagnosis, both as a dyslexic and a poet.

When Sofia was twelve, she wrote a vivid poem called 'Resolution', which began:

> I shall take off my dyslexic coat
> And run away in my poetry dress,

But last week, she wrote this, a poem where she is still the outsider, still cut off from books and the things which help, but where she is also potent, mysterious, full of brains and hurt: surely, a poem about dyslexia, and how it is not, after all, something to be taken off, but rather part of her essence and her gift.

Learning Difficulty

Times I felt like a blackberry bush, sitting
in the corner hiding blue brains

darker than bruises. Times I taught myself
to be content with being alone, myself

my own crutch. Times spent smelling
pink and blue words. I remember talking

to the dark. I don't remember the bookshelves
any more, but I feel the crates

of ordered pages standing upright like soldiers.
In the place I wasn't allowed to go were the things

I really needed, the slug pellets to keep
albatrosses away from the primroses. I'm recalling

me pushing my hair back with my glasses
that sat on my head like a robin, us

both out of place.

Chris and Janie's Code

Janie and Chris are eleven and have Autism Spectrum
Disorder. They know this: they are fully certified and state-
mented; they will tell you all about it freely. They are
cheerful, frank children in general: shouty, active, unselfconsciously odd. When we fill in the form for a poetry
competition, they both seek out and tick 'other' for their
gender. This seems spot on; though they both wear skirts
and have long, thick hair, it is somehow very hard to identify them as girls. There are too many things they are not
doing, indefinable ways of walking and sitting and talking
they are not mimicking: codes that neurotypical eleven-
year-old girls must simply pick up, and that neurotypical
I must somehow expect. When, still filling in the form, they
flick through the lists of 'country of origin', I feel there
should be an 'other' for that too: ASD Land.

They are devoted to each other and have been, appar-
ently, since early in primary school; many of their poems
are about their friendship, and the ones that aren't are
carefully dedicated to each other. Janie is more sociable

and outgoing than Chris; Chris is more gifted in the classic ASD subjects such as Maths, and they work as a team at all times. The school acknowledges and enables this relationship, always timetabling them together. They are right: a friendship like this is very unusual for ASD kids, and defends them against many things, especially the undeniable fact that no one else wants to be friends with them. It's not that they are not clever, kind, or warm: they are. But they are entering the teenage years, when sociability is everything, and Janie and Chris can't read social codes at all. Even in class, the jokes not got, the gestures not reciprocated, all the small, intuitive, empathetic moves which Janie and Chris can't make and can't learn make them jarring company.

Probably, more than an hour a week would irritate me, too, but for that hour, I like them very much. They are easy to deal with if I am very clear: for instance, they don't pick up subtle signals about when to stop talking but heed me absolutely when I tell them explicitly that they are breaking the rules of my lesson. If I set them a task they will stick at it, without deviating, for hours, and never ask why. This is fun. Once, I set them the absurdly abstruse and difficult exercise of imitating the half-rhyme couplets in Paul Muldoon's 'Sushi' (leotard/leopard, magnetized/East), then forgot about them while a sixth-former had a UCAS crisis. By the time I remembered, late, a full ninety minutes afterwards, they had turned out one hundred couplets in the form, mostly about mythic animals. If their verses had had a plot, or an emotional thrust, I could have sent them to the *Poetry Review*.

When we do some work on imaginary dictionaries and making up words, Janie and Chris go off their heads with excitement. They have, it seems, been working on a private language for some years. They hastily write me a poem in it and show it to the group; it looks like runes, carved deeply into the A4 with biros. The code goes deep into the page, explains Chris, because it is based on letters drawn on top of each other, in an order only the two of them understand. The five lines in front of us represent nearly four hundred words. The pretty, made-up faces of the Poetry Group girls are a picture of bafflement under their soft curls and plaits, and it flashes on me that it is remarkable, what two girls can achieve in a bedroom when they are free of all thoughts about personal adornment.

'But,' says dyslexic Sofia, who has dropped in to help, 'how can we understand your poem?' Because she sees no point in codes, per se. There are enough impenetrable ones around her already; she wants meaning.

'We'll translate it,' says Janie, and she reads it aloud, in her shouty, toneless voice, Chris supplying notes. The poem is about a girl who is afraid. She is afraid that when she speaks no one will understand her. She is silent, and her fear grows. In the night, it turns into a tree which covers her whole house and window. Then her friend comes and calls to her. She calls back, and together their voices melt the tree.

'Nice poem,' says Sofia. 'I still don't get why you wrote it like that.'

'We could only write it like that,' says Janie. 'That's our code.'

'Great,' I say, shutting down the discussion, initiating applause.

Though I don't intuitively understand Janie and Chris's poetic impulse, really, any more than Sofia does. But then, I don't appreciate Lydia Davis, really, or L=A=N=G=U=A=G=E poets, or most of the Oulipian movement. These writers' relationship to language is the opposite of mine, as Janie and Chris's poem is the opposite of Sofia's. To have ASD is to be a hyper-processor, so while Sofia and I suffer from not being able to put one thing in front of another, from not being able to force our wide cup of perception down our narrow pipe of process, Janie and Chris suffer from the opposite. Everything in their minds is processed, ordered, and codified too fast; they don't have time to read emotions, can't understand things that are resistant to code, such as facial expressions. Janie and Chris like system, reference, encyclopaedic knowledge, and myths, lots of it; their creative impulse is to make a code of their own. Sofia and I like contemplating small tangles of images, personal emotions, and concrete references. We circle these things on top of each other, making a unit, a moment, a tunnel to another person, a small home on the large earth.

But Janie and Chris are poets just as Sofia is, and I can recognize their system-building, code-making impulse in the creativity of many contemporary and classic poets. They remind me of William Blake, often, and make me wonder if that perverse, difficult polymath with his no-torious bad manners, love of the abstruse, and determinedly autodidact learning, also had ASD. It is easy to imagine Janie and Chris, forty years on, sunbathing nude in the back garden like Blake and his wife, greeting visitors wearing only a hat, showing off a printing press for their impossible code. Janie and Chris make my relationship with Blake easier, in fact, because I have only ever loved bits of his work and have baulked and worried about the indigestible epics like 'Jerusalem'. In my mind, now, I tell him, frankly and openly as I tell Janie and Chris: my brain works differently from yours, William, and I just can't get the stuff about Swedenborg. But you go on, WB. You go right ahead.

About Being Well

Lianne, Danielle, Susie, Kristell, Courtney, and Dawud

That poor people are less well than rich people is a lesson you can teach yourself any afternoon in a doctor's surgery or an urban supermarket. How profoundly poverty affects children though, how much more often they have chronic illnesses, accidents, and disabilities than their richer peers, is a lesson that takes years to learn.

Lianne's Biscuit and Courtney's Dance

Thursday afternoon: my Inclusion group. It has taken a while to get us all writing quietly. Now Tia has settled in the corner where she insists on putting herself, and Susie has her thumb in her mouth, sucking in thought, and pens are conscientiously scratching across papers, and even Olivia, who gets the shakes, has stopped and Kristell, at last, has her arm around her work, her fluffy pen scribbling.

'But,' bursts out Lianne, apropos of nothing. 'You are all thin. All of you. I'm the only fat one.'

'No, I'm the fat one,' shrieks Kristell, all peace lost, little hands flying, shakes restored. 'Look at me! I'm all fat. So fat!'

'You go out and in,' says Lianne. 'Out and in. Curves. I'm fat.'

Actually, Lianne is fat. It worries me, how much she has to haul up the stairs to get to class, how she arrives gasping for breath.

'Shush,' I say, 'Lianne. Write your poem.'

'No,' says Lianne. 'My poem is about being fat, and I can't write it here because no one else is fat. Look, Tia and Kristell are curvy, Olivia' (resentful stare) 'is anorexic. Susie is just so thin, and Miss' – she gazes at me – 'Miss is the thinnest person her age I've ever seen.'

'I'm not,' I say. 'Do be quiet.'

I cannot be the thinnest woman Lianne has ever seen. I am a very ordinary shape for a middle-class woman of fifty: a bit heavy on the hips, but waist carefully preserved with front crawl and Pilates. I know this is an ordinary shape because I check myself, anxiously, frequently, against my middle-class peers, the women I work with and work out with, and this is how we roll.

But of course, Lianne is not middle-class. Lianne comes from an extended family of women – mothers and grand-mothers and aunts – who are all fat. I know them by sight because there are cousins and siblings throughout the school, and the older generation turn up a lot, both to the trouble meetings – counsellors, exclusions – and to plays and concerts, for their children are sweet and performative and musical as well as trouble. When the whole tribe come to the play, or to see Lianne sing, they fill a row of the hall like a horizon loaded with rain clouds.

So maybe I really am the thinnest middle-aged woman Lianne has ever seen. Maybe Lianne is telling me that she hasn't seen many middle-class women, and that I and my middle-class waist make her feel uncomfortable and judged: the way I feel when I change in the university pool in a crowd of muscled twenty-year-olds.

I few years back, I taught Lianne's cousin, Danielle – or is it aunt? (The generations are blurred.) She was thought to be very bright, as Lianne is: a bit special. Being special was why both girls were sent to me in Poetry Group, or at least, that was the reason we gave them. On paper, they were both having 'an intervention to preclude and circumvent the effects of a very deprived background on a student with strong academic potential as evidenced by Level 5 Year 6 SAT results'. We want Lianne, and wanted Danielle, to do really well, in other words. To fulfil their academic potential and go to university. To not fall into the same trap as so many disadvantaged children, and fail at secondary school after starting well at primary school.

Lianne is a lot more interested in writing than her cousin. Danielle's poems tended to start well, then fizzle into something not all that special, perhaps because she was always too busy to develop anything; after all, she was also in all the top sets, and playing Sandy in our school production of *Grease*, and star of the netball team. Her boyfriend, who came constantly into her conversation and poems, was a free runner, and on the weekends Danielle would go with him, and run up the towers in the city centre, and all over the car park at the back of the station.

In one way, though, Danielle really was special: she was exquisitely pretty in the dark and elfin, Audrey Hepburn mode. She knew it, too; she was always finding occasion to take off her clothes and expose her pale, beautifully turned limbs. She declared, for instance, that it was easier to write poems in shorts, and would wriggle out of her uniform in the corner of the classroom to change. Between lessons, she was always demonstrating dance moves out by the sports hall, skirt ridden up to her crotch. 'Poseur', the kids called her, but she tossed her head, uncaring, sure of her talent. When I left school in the summer evenings, Danielle always seemed to be perched up on the gate, one hand in her lap like the Little Mermaid, boys and girls gazing up at her as she gesticulated and chattered, her little denim jacket pert on her slim shoulders, all potential and shiny pale lip gloss.

Nothing bad happened to Danielle. She didn't take drugs or drop out of school or turn to crime – but somehow the winter she turned fifteen she lost the free-running boyfriend and gave up dance. And somehow the following spring she slipped out of the top sets, and the summer after that, she didn't get great GCSEs; and somehow, after two years of sitting around in the sixth form, she failed her A Levels. Somehow, somehow, she missed all those ambitious targets we had for her in the same way she never finished her poems, in the way white, poor students so persistently do less well than they ought, as if they were being pulled downwards by an invisible current.

And all the time, as if refusing middle-class food along with middle-class ambition, Danielle put on weight. At first, she didn't seem to notice, and continued to strip off at every opportunity, continuing to pose on gateposts and desks, ignoring the soft pads adhering to her sculptural limbs like clay. At first, she still wore the little denim jacket, her new bosom protruding ever more bulbously beneath it. Then it got too small to go over her arms and she wore it like a shawl over her shoulder. Then, she discarded it, and wore bovver boots and leggings and smock tops and was fat.

The last time I saw Danielle, she was twenty and had come in to help with the school play. She was standing behind the lead, a slim child in a leotard, and I mistook her for her own mother. I was surprised how hurt I was to see it. It wasn't the flesh so much as the loss of grace; now she stood the way her mother stood, legs apart to hold the bulk, stomach out, arms awkward and ashamed. I thought of the poised girl she had been, and the phrase *she got above herself* came to my mind. Danielle had been brought down from that moment of beauty, subsumed in the women around her like a nymph tugged down by hounds. It only took seven years.

'Shut up,' says Tia, now, trying to write as ever. 'Shut up, Lianne. Have a biscuit. Have a biscuit and write your poem.'

'Yeah,' I say, 'go on, Lianne. You've made a good start.' And I pass the biscuits. Lianne always makes a good start; then, too often, something happens. Shouting about being fat is just one of the potential disasters.

Tia has a biscuit, too. I don't, because this New Year, when my middle-class swimming group announced competitive resolutions to give up sugar, carbs, cake, I came up with the simplest: to give up lunch. And I'm sticking to it, so I'm hungry now, this Thursday afternoon as I talk to Lianne. Lianne is stuffing fig rolls, my favourite, into her pretty fat face, and it is very hard indeed not to have one. I can manage it, I think, in the same way that I can manage to finish a poem, because I am middle-class. Because, since I was a tiny child, I have been taught to wait for long-term goals: for dinner instead of a snack, for good exam passes instead of a party, for university instead of a job, for a job instead of a baby, and – very important, this – the promised rewards have duly been given to me. Now, I am able to think, or more to the point, to feel and believe, that the long-term reward of thinness is better than the short-term one of a fig roll. I think it's worth it. I think I'm worth it.

But Lianne doesn't think she's worth much. This she keeps establishing as she writes poem after poem in which she is abandoned by stepfathers and boyfriends and friends. It's in the way she writes, too, in those good starts which falter, in the way she can't draft, can't bear to look at what she has written, the way she downloads and copies work from the internet. She's like her cousin, really. Lianne and Danielle come from the same loving but chaotic backgrounds. Rewards and treats come, but irregularly and irrationally. Neither of them has had the experience of waiting for things and then being well rewarded for waiting. They take the short term because the long term has let them down over and over again. They can't refuse biscuits any more than they can study. They can't believe in university any more than they can believe in thinness, or themselves.

'I wish,' says Lianne, eating the biscuit, and it is a familiar theme, 'I wish I was anorexic. Like Olivia. Bulimia, you don't get no sympathy.'

'Olivia ain't anorexic,' says Tia. 'She said so, didn't she? And we give you lots of sympathy. Now shut up.'

Olivia is in the room, but she says nothing. Olivia is on strong anti-depressants. Her shakes are constant and very hard to control; we have to use a carpeted classroom so that the tables don't rattle. She has been on high doses of what she calls her 'meds' for a couple of years, since a serious suicide attempt. She says she hates them, that they stop her from feeling, but also that she needs them, they insulate her from feelings. She also says, and I believe her because she is only thin, not starved looking, that whatever Lianne says, she doesn't have a food problem as such; she just finds it hard to unclench enough to swallow. Her poems are written in sharp, high, oblique handwriting, very fast, and reveal sharpened, heightened slices of a tortured world. Olivia stays thin enough to slip away, to disappear through her own door.

'I don't actually know any anorexics,' muses Kristell, reaching for another biscuit. 'Not in this school.'

I don't, either, not in our school, though I do worry sometimes about Zosia. She is the cleverest girl in the sixth form, intent on medical school, and carrying the expectations of a poor Polish family in her carefully packed school bag. She is also blonde and very pretty and slim: recently, too slim. But Zosia tries too hard to be in control, and anorexia is a disease of control. That's why it is a middle-class disorder; why it is rampant in the academic girls' school up the road. Bulimia, on the other hand, that expression of chaos, self-hatred, and mixed messages, is common in our school, and so, epidemically, is self-harm.

'I used to be skinny,' says Kristell, now thoroughly disrupted. 'Not no more.'

She did. When Kristell arrived in Year 9, she had a bosomy, curvy figure with a tiny waist and pretty ankles. She also had huge, fringed brown eyes, a pouting, sorrowful, half-open mouth, lush, waist-length brunette curls, and a downy, newly hatched quality altogether. She looked like trouble, was my first thought.

And she was trouble too. I taught her English set, and she disrupted it. She wasn't noisy, as such, herself – she had a soft, breathy voice to match the Bambi lashes and fresh mouth – but noise followed her, arose around her like thorns around an enchanted princess. 'It ain't me!' was one of her cries. 'Miss, I ain't doing it on purpose.'

And she wasn't. She wore less make-up than many of the other girls, sported no special variation of the school uniform. But each morning she got out of bed and brushed out her cloud of princess hair, and there she was, locked in a puddle of pretty, a bubble of trouble, and she couldn't get out of it any more than a fly can get out of milk.

But Kristell herself, when you got to know her, was very intelligent and desperate to please, especially when it came to writing. She loved poems; they made her little hands shake with pleasure. She wanted to write, too, but it made her nervous. What if she wrote the wrong thing? 'Miss!' she would say, in her husky voice. 'I'm getting my anxiety.' Her lip would quiver and her nose wrinkle. I'd send her to the quiet corner; I'd let her put on her headphones. Her poems were usually about loss, especially the loss of 'innocence' (her favourite word) and childhood. Once she started, she wrote most earnestly, her fluffy-top pen, bright pink, bobbing along the paper.

Once, when she complained that she couldn't get any peace to finish a poem, because it was so noisy, boys were bombarding her with paper balls, whispering her name, taking her drafts from the bin and reading them aloud, and she begged me to explain why, I said: 'It's because you're very beautiful, and they are trying to get your attention. Because they like you.'

Her pretty face crumpled in pain. She dropped her pen. 'Oh no, Miss,' she said, 'you got that one wrong. They hate me.' And when I demur: 'No, Miss, really, that's hate. They hate me.'

Kristell already had, then, at fourteen – she showed me under her school shirt – a contraceptive implant in her arm, but no steady boyfriend. There was trouble in her family; that's why they moved town, why she arrived in our school mid-year. Just a few months later, she had a sort of breakdown. Now she is back, shakily, in school, but she has bleached her beautiful hair a coarse yellow and cut it short. She is on anti-depressants. She has put on a great deal of weight, so that the pretty figure is blurred, so that she looks like her mum, so that she has breached her bubble, so that she is not such a target of notice and noise.

Now Kristell sits with Lianne and Tia and writes about assault and rape and arm-slashing and helplessness. She is barely fifteen: a child. I think she was right to tell me that the boys' attention was a form of hate; it was, and so was my attitude to her, so was the attitude of our entire society, the attitude that identifies the disruption as coming from the young girl, not the gazing man, that attributes power to such a powerless person.

I have not yet tried to explain the word 'patriarchal' to this group. Kristell still likes to write, and to read out her poems in her soft, husky voice. The dark eyes gazing out of the fat pink cheeks are still so very lovely.

Janine performed a similar act of self-sabotage. Janine from the Inclusion Unit. Not that I knew her very long, for she had no intention of staying in the IU, and still less of writing a poem. She sat with her arms mulishly folded, rolling her eyes at my every pronouncement. She muttered continually except when I asked for contributions, when she set her teeth and stared at the ceiling. Asked to write, she outright refused. She wanted a 'proper lesson'. Miss B gently pointed out that she had been thrown out of most of those. In the end, before she took the rest of the group with her, we allowed her to flounce off to a table where she tried to draw attention to herself by putting her feet on it.

She wasn't a pretty girl, even by the standards of the IU, even if she wasn't making a terrible face. She was fat, a swathe of freckly flesh bulging out from her collar, blurring her jaw line, giving her premature double chins. Her hair had been dyed purple, a cruel, chemical colour, and there were lines of studs in her ears and nose. She was wearing a long-sleeved shirt, though it was summer, the way Kristell always does, the way girls do when they are scarred.

Miss B sees me watching. Look, she says, and puts a school record sheet under my nose. It's for a Year 10 girl with a slim neck and cheekboney face and the most beautiful warm blonde hair flowing over her shoulders: dolly hair, little girl hair, princess hair, like Kristell's. Miss B puts her finger under the name. It's Janine.

Four months ago, she whispers, as the kids have finally settled to their work. Look, she's got a great report and everything.

What happened? I write on Miss B's pad.

She was raped, Miss B writes back. And when I look up at her, startled, she whispers: Makes perfect sense, doesn't it?

Now Susie says, 'You've got to stop like, moaning on about it, Lianne. About what you're eating, what you're not eating, all that. It's actually really boring? It's like, disempowering?'

Susie quite often uses words like 'disempowering', and also always uses upspeak. Susie has her own YouTube channel in which she talks about empowerment in upspeak while wearing her underwear. Susie is blonde with long legs and a slim waist and wide eyes, and she layers on shiny make-up in such quantities that on the YouTube channel she looks at least twenty-five, or maybe no age at all, maybe like a form of artificial life generated by YouTube.

Susie has many, many subscribers; and the child protection officer is a little stumped. Is it empowering to talk about empowerment while making an object of yourself in your pants? Certainly, Kim Kardashian, icon of our age, gives out the message that it is, and so does Victoria Beckham, and even, in a subtle, double-edged way, Taylor Swift. Susie makes money out of it, £300 a month. She is very sure she is winning, profiting from the male gaze, while Kristell is losing.

I don't tackle her on it. My own view is: probably best not to invest yourself in the male gaze, probably a better idea to turn on the Lily Allen and have a little dance with your girlfriends; I think, if you must make a YouTube video let it not be in your pants – but then I would, wouldn't I? I have never been thin and blonde; I have always had other sources of power in my life.

And anyway, I like Susie. She has such oomph. Her current poem is about her mother, about a moment when she was young and lovely and photographed for a magazine. When she could do anything, says Susie. And then she lost it. So Susie may have some grip on the male gaze, after all.

In her chosen corner, under her huddling arm, Tia is writing another poem for her sister. Tia's sister died of heroin addiction last year, and Tia lives with her dad and her gran because her mum is also an addict. Tia copes, everyone agrees, remarkably well. Not only does she keep out of any kind of trouble or substance abuse herself, but she works hard in school, and is universally well liked: kind, thoughtful, calm, friendly, and balanced. Tia also has a steady boyfriend, but she never writes about that relationship. Instead, she writes over and over again about her anxiety, about her pain and mourning, and about heroin, about whether she too will be addicted. And what does such a waif look like? Well, not like a waif. Tia is broad faced, solid, and working on making herself more solid. Mum-shaped; not heroin addict-shaped. She grabs the biscuits and stuffs in two at once as if to comfort herself, or maybe to shut herself up.

And that makes me think of Courtney. Courtney brought herself to Poetry Group for a focused term of writing two years after her brother was killed in a horrible accident. Courtney was bright, an accurate and fluent writer, and marvellously direct. In my group, she wrote a set of elegies, and then took them away with her; she didn't want them published, she didn't want to redraft them. They were not, honestly, as good as they could have been, but Courtney was satisfied with them. She had come, she told me clearly and calmly, on the advice of her counsellor and as part of her grief journey, and now she was done and going to focus on dance and sport.

This she did: she captained every school team through her sixth form and would have been on some county teams too, except every year she put on another ten pounds or so of fat on her small, strong frame, and slowed herself down too much to win at hurdles.

Most girls would have been put off dance, that most mirroring and merciless of disciplines, but not Courtney.

Not only did she dance herself, but she also put on, in her last term, an ambitious show for younger students, and choreographed the dance section. Her dance, she announced with characteristic straightforwardness, was all about empowerment for girls, and being proud of your body. A familiar message, and one which, as the usual medley of well-worn pop songs came up on the sound system, we all settled back to take with a pinch of salt.

The music was naff, and Courtney's dancers, mostly girls of about thirteen in leggings and T-shirts, were all shapes and sizes, and limited in their range. It was satisfying, though, to see a dance in which nothing nymph-like or delicate occurred; Courtney had built a simple narrative about building and lifting, parting and coming together. At the end of the show, Courtney herself, with her heavy stocky body, performed a duet with one of the only boys involved: tall, strong, African Jonathon. In the dance, they courted each other, quarrelled, parted, made up: simple, strong, equal manoeuvres. At the curtain call Courtney, bowing in the spotlight, was lit by her own work and her own vision, and she looked beautiful, and as if she felt she was beautiful. As if she had taken herself somewhere, which she had, and really was empowered, which she was.

I never felt like that at fifteen. I never saw beyond my acne and my hips. Even as a young woman, I never managed to like myself, or see myself except as men might see me. Looking at the fifteen-year-olds before me now, I feel the waste of it all: all the youth and happiness being spoilt, for I do not think that one of them is happy like

Courtney, not even Susie, because if she were, why would she feel such a need to perform? And the waste comes from me, too, from my commodifying, snobbish, patriarchal gaze.

'You all look beautiful to me,' I say, making it true as I say it, pushing aside the prejudices which hedge and besiege my gaze. 'You look beautiful because you're young. You've got to enjoy that.'

Maybe they hear me. Lianne smiles; Susie says, yeah. Tia says, 'Thank you, Miss,' conscientiously. Kristell says, 'My mum always says that. I dunno though. Dunno if I believe her.'

Dawud's Sister

Dawud is in the sixth form. He is supposed to be doing A Level with me, but he has not attended class for a fortnight or handed in his coursework, so we are having a conference. I'm prepared to be annoyed with Dawud; with his trendy lumberjack shirt and tight jeans, elaborately shaved side-burns and earring, he seems a bit Jack-the-Lad to me, a bit cocksure. I get the exam syllabus out and make him read it. I explain that my deadline is a real deadline, even if my course is called 'creative', and if he doesn't hand in the work it really might have the effect of his failing the exam. He doesn't reply, though, and as I talk on I have the feeling of not being heard at all, of my words flowing over the coiffed, blue-black quiff of hair he has bent into his small ringed hands.

'I've got a problem at home,' he says, to the table. 'I had

to stay and help my mum because she doesn't speak English.'

This happens quite a lot to the Asian girls. It doesn't happen to their brothers nearly so often, not unless they are the only person available. 'Is your dad away?' I ask, suspiciously.

'In Pakistan,' says Dawud.

'So you're the man of the house?' I know this is inevitable. It still annoys me, though, the boys lording it over their mums.

He nods. He drums his fingers on the table, looks up at the ceiling. The problem, he says, suddenly, angrily, is that his sister can't get out of bed, or even shower herself, and his mum has to be with her all day; she can't cook, shop, do anything.

'Well, she's probably ill,' I say, 'your sister.'

'Yes,' says Dawud, 'she's really, really ill.'

'OK,' I say, softening. 'Sorry about that.'

Dawud pauses, eyes down. He's a bad colour, yellow-pale. Then I see he has tears in his eyes.

'Really sorry, Dawud,' I say. 'What's wrong with your sister?'

And then this story arrives. It takes a while, and comes out backwards, but Dawud keeps at it, talking without prompts. He seems to want to tell me, or perhaps, finding himself in a quiet room at last, he is trying to piece it together for himself. His sister has an unnamed illness – no fevers or rashes or anything like that, no broken limbs, but she can't get out of bed. She is the middle of his three sisters, younger than him, just fifteen. It started last year when they all went back to Pakistan to celebrate the marriage of his older sister. They had a great time, but one night, while the family were all enjoying themselves at a festival, the middle sister stayed out too late, and – this bit makes Dawud sigh, and pluck at his quiff – a *jinn*, a spirit, became jealous of the whole family and their wealth, and got into his sister's body and made her ill.

'Do you believe that?' I ask. 'About the *jinn*?'

'Miss,' says Dawud. '*Jinn* are Islam, yeah? They're in the Koran. And like, what I'm telling you is what they told me, yeah?'

Jinn are in the Koran, I know that already. I've heard about them from students from Islamic countries: from Albania to Somalia, Afghanistan to Syria, but especially from Pakistanis and Bengalis. *Jinn* are spirits, part of the unseen world, but have a physical reality on the earth too. Some of them are angels and some of them are demons, for *jinn* can choose, just like people, to be good or bad, to accept Islam or not. Some *jinn* are neither good nor bad but just themselves: mischievous, jealous, manifesting themselves as small fires, minor illnesses, cold breezes, mental breakdown. *Jinn* attack people who are exiled from their home country, especially when they go home for a visit. Disproportionately, *jinn* attack young women: new brides, younger sisters, unmarried women – whole classrooms of girls, sometimes.

'Miss,' says Dawud, clearly seeing the scepticism in my eyes. 'I was born here. In England? Me, at the time, in Pakistan? I was like, yeah, she's got a bug, she's eaten something, she'll be fine when we get back to England.'

But his sister wasn't fine when they came home to England; she stayed lethargic and apathetic. She stayed in bed all day, then started to get pains in her legs, to find it hard to breathe. They went to the doctor, many times, but nothing helped. She was supposed to start Year 11, finish her GCSEs. She attended for a day or two, then stopped. Weeks went by. And then her parents took her to London.

'To find a *raqi*,' says Dawud. 'To perform *ruqyah*. Like, our tradition. Healing?'

There are a surprising number of *raqi* in England. In London, especially. I've heard about them from African as well as Indian students. What they do varies, but some of it is violent. Some of it involves sitting on the possessed person, shouting at them, shaking them, for days and hours. There have been deaths.

'An exorcism?' I suggest. 'To get rid of the *jinn*?' Dawud licks his lips, shakes his shoulders, slides back into his street voice.

'That's when we found out about the *jinn*, to be honest with you?' says Dawud. 'The *raqi*? He said it was a *shaytan*, a bad *jinn*. And he explained about how it got to her? The festival, and how the *jinn* got jealous of us, and all that.'

I don't need to express any doubts about this: Dawud clearly feels them already. He goes over and over his father's decision to go to the *raqi*, justifying it. The *raqi* was a really good one, everyone said. He was really expensive. Everyone said it had to happen. That's why his dad did it. To help. Nothing was helping his sister.

'But did it help?' I ask.

'I don't know,' says Dawud, miserably. 'I don't know. They took her away for three days, I didn't see her.'

That was three weeks ago. Now, Dawud's sister cannot eat or walk. Now she screams in pain all the time. Now she lies hunched on the bed and says the sheets are tearing at her skin, the mattress is battering her bones. The doctor has come, several times. There have been dozens of tests. He's talking about hospital.

'Miss,' says Dawud, 'I think the *raqi* made her worse.'

'You know,' I say at this point, 'that I have to tell everyone about this? About your sister and everything you've told me. I have to tell the Deputy Head?'

'No,' says Dawud. 'I already did. Two days ago. As soon as my dad went to Pakistan? I told the school. I told everyone. Social workers? Everyone. And they all came to our house, they're crawling all over it. Everyone in our house, saying stuff. My mum doesn't understand any of it, that's why I have to be there? She doesn't understand the words they're saying. That's what I'm telling you, Miss.'

Telling the school and the social work department was a huge, brave thing for Dawud to do, and it has done very little good. Later, I'll add my voice to those listing concerns about the family; for now, I work with Dawud on his writing assignment. We make a list of words that the doctors don't understand: *tasbih*, prayers counted off on a rosary; *shaytan*, a demon, a *jinn* that has refused Islam; *Koran Sharif*, the holy book – and another list of words that his mother doesn't understand: *ME, Lyme disease, leukaemia, psychological, schizophrenia, section, care.* We arrange them in a sort of dictionary form, alphabetized. It becomes a poem.

'You know when you went to Pakistan that first time,' I ask, as we work, 'for your older sister's wedding. When you met the *jinn*? Was that to get her engaged? I mean, your younger sister?'

And it was. An informal contract. To an older man. This has nothing to do with anything.

The poem worked out well, but that was the last time I saw Dawud. After that, his family returned to Pakistan.

About What I Think I
Am Doing

Jason, Aimee, Heya, and Shakila

In therapy, you articulate your feelings; in poetry, you do the same. As a result, poetry and therapy often get confused; there's even something called Poetry Therapy. When I'm asked about this – on stage at a literary festival, for example – I usually make a distinction first: poetry is for making art, therapy is for making you feel better; poetry is for the reader, therapy is for you; then hastily resort to jokes. If poetry is therapy, I ask, why are poets such difficult characters? Why do they drink so, and squabble, and pick their emotional wounds in public? Why am I, having written so many poems, still bad-tempered and irrational and anxious? What, in short, do poets know?

Usually, I get a laugh. But this line does not go down so well when applying for jobs or funding for my work. These days, money for the arts, especially for young people, is often raised by bids to multiple agencies, bids which will not be successful unless they promise psychological as well as educational benefit. There is a sort of philanthropic market value in uncovering trauma in disadvantaged young people and getting them to write about it. Creative

Writing merely as a part of English, on the other hand, won't get a grant; writing has to change a young person's life, 'turn them round'. A poet can't be just a teacher; she has to be a guru, or at least a psychotherapist.

When I begin working as a writer in schools, I find it difficult to make these sorts of promises. In the classroom I still think of myself as a teacher, albeit one with a specialism, and tend to behave like one too, always focusing on reading, dishing out detentions for the back row. I'm uneasy talking about psychological turnaround; I have no training in that. I'm more confident with targets of more accurate spelling and wider reading. I want to improve.

So, the year I start in the Inclusion Unit, I take myself on a two-day course for writers in schools in a bid to up my skills. The course, in a smart venue in Manchester, is led by experienced writers, not teachers, and this is an important selling point. Writers, we are told over the two days, must hold on to our special 'real' status in schools, so that we can transmit our 'real' magic to children. I am unsure about this. It's tiresome for teachers to work with 'magic' people, because then they have to be the straight man. Besides, there are not many published writers on the course. I can all too easily imagine the feelings of a teacher who has an aspiring performance poet roll into their Year 10 and tell them to forget all about exams on the grounds that he, and not Miss, is 'real'.

But it's good for young people to be told they are doing something special, I tell myself. There is magic in writing, of course there is, I remind myself. Beware of being a sourpuss, I add. I go to some interesting drama workshops, and one from a helpful psychotherapist. Then I attend the class I really need: the one about story-writing. I've realized I have surprisingly little idea of how to go about this, and it is always in demand. An enthusiastic young novelist is sharing her best lesson, one she uses regularly, by teaching it to the group. She is asking us some special questions, and we are writing answers as honestly and unselfconsciously as we can. The questions seem open and easy at first – which place do you think of as home? – but move swiftly on to the heavy duty. Who have you treated badly in your life? What one thing do you most regret? What would you change if you could?

I am writing . . . but I can't write here what I am writing. I am in tears at the memory. I was in tears at the time: back in a trauma, an unhealed memory, helpless. I'd just dropped into it as I was answering the questions; then I found myself writing it, out of control. We are asked to read, and I use all my journalistic skills to invent a cover story, a fictional answer. I'm sweating. Several other people round the table are also upset. The novelist seems to think this is a good thing, that this is how you start a story, that by doing this, we are opening ourselves to good writing. But I'm closing myself, rapidly. I score out everything on my paper, wordless, speechless.

Later, I chew over the things I failed to say: for example, that this is not how any trained teacher would behave and maybe teachers know stuff; that you cannot, you must not, ask young people questions like that unless you are a counsellor and have the training and resources and back-up to deal with the disclosure of abuse or the uncontrollable grief or simply the severe upset in the middle of a school day which might come of them; that yes, writing may well have its origins in trauma, but it is not our business to provoke or suggest that process; that writers must do their own provoking, in their own time, when they are ready; that the Freudian idea that it is healing simply to speak of a trauma cannot be right, because it cannot be empowering to anyone to feel as helpless as those questions made me feel.

So I go away from the conference even more the classroom teacher, and less the classroom writer, than when I began. In fact, I have a new set of worries: about trauma, writing, and disclosure, and beyond that, in the marketing of disclosure. I'm not sure what I will do about them in the future, but I am resolved that whatever it is, I will never make a child feel as I did in that room.

Jason's Skull

I promised myself always to be a teacher in class, and to focus on art, and excellence, and the production of good writing. Stories come from stories, poems from poems, not from digging up trauma: this is what I tell everyone. I vowed never to use any technique that began with psychological probing, never to ask a direct biographical question, or ever to press anyone for true information. I would always begin a workshop with some reading, something to lean on and imitate and hide behind. I would make sure always to offer the possibility of a fiction: the use of the third person, for example, or a science fiction frame.

And I stuck to these promises. I stick to them now. But, as I did with Priya and Priti and their novel about the American camp, I often found myself asking students to be *real*: to use actual details from their actual lives, even when – especially when – they were constructing a fiction. This is because personal observation and good writing almost always coincide; they make fresh images in the mind and on the page. Drawing from life also short-circuits cliché production and basic mistakes, like Priti's motorized canoe. Most writers know this; this is why we chant mantras such as 'write about what you know'; 'show, don't tell'; and 'write the poem only you can write' in Creative Writing classes. We mean: please don't regurgitate another teen novel; no more summer camps and canoes, we all have heard enough received versions of the world; your own, however eccentric, will be more interesting.

Good writing always starts from good reading. Joe Brainard's *I Remember* was one of my favourite models: a whole book made up of short, disconnected paragraphs about growing up gay in forties America, each segment beginning 'I remember'; each hilarious, moving, and juicy with sensual particulars. It's a shape that gives importance to the small, real details of a life, the parts that do not seem grand enough even to be remembered, but somehow are central. It's also a shape that asks to be copied, and, liberatingly, is: there are lots of 'I remember' versions in bookshops and on the web, written by published writers as well as students.

And so, in a Year 11 Inclusion group with a few tough boys in it, I read out first a few Brainard paragraphs, the cleanest I could find, then a longer 'I remember' piece by the poet Paul Farley. The group drank down Farley's account of a working-class childhood in Liverpool like a forbidden beer, and after a lengthy discussion of childhood adventures and crimes, and much enjoining from me to focus on the detail and think about the senses, Jason, a freckly, squinty boy with a rap sheet as long as his arm, waved his pen in the air, and scribbled down a series of shocking memories: the time he got drunk and banged his head on the wall, but couldn't feel the pain; buying cigarette lighters in the car boot sale and setting them off like bombs, but the explosion was never enough; the time he was sent into the police station by older boys to take the blame for a crime and he studied himself in the two-way mirror, trying to find the right shape; the time he had his head hacked open in a fight; how he couldn't cry until he looked in the mirror and saw his skull.

All of the moments he had chosen were about being stunned; about blows to the head and the mind and how the brain processes them, or rather, doesn't, how it holds them as trauma. His language was clean, simple, economical, and when, at the end of the session, Jason read the poem to the group, they were, appropriately, stunned.

I passed Jason's poem up the line. It went all the way, generating (stunning) excitement in everyone who read it: the Head Teacher, the writing project manager, and the project's funders. So much excitement, in fact, that the project manager printed it on a postcard which was passed to me at a literary party in London, where I stared at it, surprised. I wasn't sure it should be here, in this smart London room, surrounded by empowered, super-clever people. It seemed small, suddenly, and terribly raw, an object of pity, a token in that market in philanthropy that made me so uneasy.

But: 'It's amazing,' said the person next to me, who I realized was a funder. 'Did you really get him to write that? I mean, he must feel so much better?'

Did he? I don't know. Jason never said. I'd heard him read the piece to large and small audiences three times; they always seemed amazed, and he always seemed pleased. He stayed in school through his GCSEs and went on to steady work, which was a good result in his circumstances. Did any of this make it a healing poem? It didn't feel healing as I read it; it just felt shocking, a shock packaged in its own poetic frame, a shock in a box.

Somehow, I didn't manage to tell the funder that Jason was healed, or that I had helped him. I folded up the postcard, and never, as requested, took it in to school or sent it to Jason. Instead, I left it in the pocket of my good coat, my London coat, and, for three years after that, I re-found it each time I went to a winter party: that harsh little trauma on stiff paper, Jason's skull. It made me feel bad. I worried that the poem exposed Jason's trauma to the world in a way he didn't understand. I worried that the poem was being read for its horror, not its cleverness. That it was a cheapening, a blurt, and I did that.

Aimee's Control

Seven years after I teach Jason, I teach Aimee. Aimee is an orphan and even in our school, even among the most disadvantaged students, this is a rare and awful misfortune. She lost both her parents in the single year between her thirteenth and fourteenth birthdays, and both to addiction. Since then, she has lived with an aunt – an inspiringly loving and supportive one – with visits to her paternal grandmother. In school, probably because of this support, she gets good grades, and is a sober, hard-working citizen, but we all worry about her, of course we do.

Aimee is also part of a special poetry group, one assembled not by me but by a PE teacher, Mr M. Mr M is young, dynamic, and shining with commitment. He is charged with the extremely difficult mission of helping the school's most disadvantaged students fulfil their academic potential. This does not mean, by and large, our migrant students, because they tend to work very hard at their studies; it means our white, poor students. It means kids like Danielle, or Simon, or Kristell – pupils who, statistically, but also in plain sight, come in from primary school as bright and high-achieving, and within a couple of years of secondary become disaffected, badly behaved non-attenders, drowning in the difficulties in their lives. Mr M is after anything, and anybody, who might help. He spots me in school, and timetables me in. His faith is not intimidating because it is so straightforward and also so undemanding. He is not after a cure, does not expect turnaround. He thinks writing things down has to be good. He thinks it will raise self-esteem, because how can it not?

He thinks doing some writing and feeling a bit special will do fine as an intention for this group, and that I will be fine in that context too, whether I am being a poet or an English teacher or a semi-counsellor.

And actually, I think, settling down in the cosy room Mr M has organized, sampling the biscuits he has provided, I agree. And so, it seems, do the students. In fact, from the very first time I sit down and read Rita Ann Higgins with them – 'Miss, that's like a real poem. Are we doing real poems in here?' – they're a joy. Each week I show them a 'real poem' and they respond with screeds of their own about the hair-raising traumas of their everyday lives: boyfriends in comas, deaths, physical and sexual abuse, abandonment. Then they share the results, and cry, buckets. I often cry too. They look forward to it all week, they say. And so do I, because however shocking the revelations, this group never give me the Shakila's head/Jason's skull feeling of being handed some live, uncontained trauma; on the contrary, we seem to have happened on a safe place, and a method of holding each other up. Maybe I am getting better at this.

Part of this is certainly the reading and listening we're doing. The group's enthusiasm for performance poetry, in particular, is huge; they actually start storing poems on their phones and bringing them to class. They value poets who look and sound like them, and who talk openly about trauma in their lives, especially Melissa Lee-Houghton, the on-the-edge Manchester poet with her tales of bodies and abandonment. We love love love Melissa Lee-Houghton, and watch and read miles of her, and one day we stumble across an interview in which she is talking about poetry and mental health. She says, frankly and simply, that she suffers from depression and poetry is not the cure for it, but that poetry can give her a way of understanding and formulating herself, both as she writes it, and as she reads herself back afterwards. It gives her some distance and some control.

The kids are mesmerized by this, and so am I. Control. Not turnaround, but control. This word has somehow never occurred to me before, in all my anxious considerations of poetry and therapy, but it seems the right one. The writing of a poem does not open the writer to a desperate blurt, or the helplessness I felt in the workshop in Manchester; rather, it orders the experience it recounts and gives the writer a grip on it. Even if they distance themselves from their experience in their writing – and self-dramatizing and exaggerating are kind of distancing, almost as much as denial is – my students are still gaining control over a torrent of experience that has often rendered them powerless. And if they dig deep, and find effective images, and make a good poem out of the truths of their lives, then that is not just control, but power. It's different from being happy; it isn't a cure for anything, but it is profoundly worth having. And actually, I don't need anyone to tell me that; I know that from my own experience. I know it for myself.

At home, I get out my good coat, and find the postcard with Jason's poem on it. It reads differently to me now. I can see he chose a good shape for his poem, and shaped each stanza artfully, so that in each is a moment of stillness which holds us in time: the blow to the head and the feeling of numbness; the arrangement of 'face' in the police station; the blankness of feeling in the glare of the explosion; the emptiness that makes you want to do it again. The tears are held till the very end, and even then, they are not real tears, but mirror tears. It isn't a merciful poem, or a healing one, but it is a very controlled one, so it cannot be a blurt. It is a very strong poem, too, strong enough to be out in the world on its own, even at a literary party. I like it, and I'm glad Jason wrote it. I'm glad I helped.

Of all the group, Aimee works the hardest as a poet. She listens like stink. She knows the importance of an image and knows that she can make them. She says, 'I've got you in my head, Miss. You say what does it look like, really, what does it smell of? All them questions.'

So what does it feel like to lose your father to heroin, Aimee? Like being an out-of-control car, a broken branch on the ground, like rubbish the seagulls are picking, says Aimee. And when, after that, your sister leaves home? Like the moment a cloud goes over the sun and your room is filled with shadow. And what does death look like? Like your mum's addict boyfriend, coming to call with a can of Stella, like the stairwell you were too young to fling him down. And where is your mother, now? In my room. In the sunset. In her scent. In my poem, Miss, safe.

Heya's Poem

Meanwhile, Shakila writes the poem about the head. It takes her the best part of three years, during which she drops in and out of Poetry Group, gets interested in politics, acquires GCSEs and A Levels and lots of words. Though never quite enough of these; at seventeen, mid-composition, she still shouts for vocabulary:

'Miss! A herb! No, a plant! It is in the mountains?'

'I dunno, Shakila, edelweiss?'

'You are joking me.'

These days, though, Shakila is computer-assisted. After a swift Google she announces: 'There! Rhubarb!'

'Rhubarb? Is rhubarb from Afghanistan?' Somehow, I associate it with English fields, but Shakila shows me the original Himalayan plant, slender pinks stalks growing from deep rock crevices, pushing their furled leaves up to the light.

'It tastes really good,' she says, 'I swear, better than this country. I ate some here – disgusting.'

And she gets on with the poem with the rhubarb in it. It has apricots in it too, and goats and mountain sheep: a lyrical account of the smallholding she and her mother lived in until she was twelve, when the Taliban closed her school and made their lives in a Hazara, Shia village intolerable. Rebuilding that village in verse is one part of Shakila's poetic project; the other part is more directly political: protests against the Taliban, the oppression of her people. The head poem is one of these, and the head itself one of a series of personal images she places against the rhetoric of the Taliban: the touch of the cheek, cold as a cloud, against the hot bloodied beards of the terrorists.

It's a magnificent poem, a triumph, but writing it doesn't change Shakila. She remains herself: trenchant and ironical, sparing and careful with emotional declarations. It is impossible to imagine her, either, saying that poetry saved her, but I think she might say it is important. I measure that importance by observing how diligent and enthusiastic she is about passing the poetry-writing habit on to others. In her last year at school, she mentors a Hazara girl so well that she too starts turning out odes and ghazals in English, and even wins a local competition. A little more cautiously, Shakila agrees to mentor a young Pashto-speaking girl from the Sunni community that had oppressed her in Afghanistan, and soon finds her prejudices swept away by the child's sweetness and untrammelled adoration.

Shakila is also keen on languages; she has Urdu as well as Persian, and some Arabic, from her journey across Asia as well as from the mosque. So when we have an Arabic poet in for the day, she drops into the workshop, and listens, and afterwards comes to speak to me about Heya, a seventeen-year-old Syrian girl very freshly arrived in school, part of a job lot of government-sponsored refugees from camps in Lebanon, Jordan, and Calais. 'Look,' she says, showing me Heya's poem, which she has photographed, pushed through Google Translate, and is working into an English version. 'Look, Miss, this is proper good.'

The poem is addressed to 'Dawn in Damascus' and is in the grand Arabic tradition, personifying dawn, asking it not to come to her house because 'the children have blood on their clothes' and the house cannot be cleaned for such a visitor. The last stanza is more conventional, a series of invocations to Allah – but these first lines are, as Shakila says, proper poetry. They make the disaster real – so real that I suspect this is a real experience, like Shakila's head.

We invite Heya to come to Poetry Group. She doesn't come. Her form teacher won't push her, either; he says that poetry upsets Heya.

But I am more confident now, after Aimee and Shakila. I don't believe that poetry will upset Heya; I think life does, and poetry can bring control. We ask Heya to come to Ghazal Club. This is a new idea of mine and Shakila's, inspired by the poet Mona Arshi. We have assembled Persian, Pashto, Urdu, and Bengali speakers. They all know a version of the word 'ghazal' and its echoing, couplet form from their own language and their own mothers, and in Ghazal Club we read and write ghazals in English. If Heya comes, we promise, she can add Arabic to the mix and listen, she can write her ghazal on flowers, or stars, or really anything pretty and cheerful at all. There will be no tears, I promise the form tutor.

And finally, Heya comes, a hesitant, small, neat figure in a long skirt, a T-shirt that says 'Big Sister' and was probably designed for a British six-year-old, and a tight black Syrian-style hijab over grand lumps of hair. Like all the Syrian kids, she is very pretty: pale skinned and dark eyed, with a sensitive mouth and a tiny, high-pitched voice. She is very interested in the ghazal. She knows it well. She has some on her phone, look. Yes, Heya certainly wants to write one. She chooses the word 'country' as her repeating word. And before you know it, she has written another deeply moving and odd poem featuring dead children, and blood, and she is in tears, and I am in trouble.

Now Heya won't come to Ghazal Club either. Don't I get it? says her form tutor. Leave her alone. Poetry just opens wounds. If so, Heya is very intent on hurting herself; she passes me in the corridor and hands me a sheet of A4 covered in purple ink. I read it and find it to be another poem, written probably in Arabic and then passed through Google Translate. The English is marvellously strange. 'My sister, you are leaving by my doorway . . . my sister, in our not-there room, wait for me'.

I show Shakila and together we do for Heya what I once did for her, what she does for her little Pashtun friend: we type up the poem and put the line breaks in. Line breaks, this is only in English, says Shakila. Probably, Heya has a rhyme in Arabic. Probably, this is an ode. But Shakila is adept at all English things now. We version Heya's work into a strong English poem. We make a couple of nice copies of it, and at lunchtime, I go down to Heya's form room, clasping them. But I am not allowed to show Heya. The form teacher will pass them on at an appropriate moment. Heya has been upset by poetry again. Did I know that she lost three sisters in Damascus? Yes, three, she has just told the form teacher. They died in front of her. A bomb fell on the house. Heya is really upset, now, and all because of that poem – but I didn't tell her to write that one, I squeak, helplessly – and I should take on board that Heya won't be writing any more poetry.

I retreat. The form teacher is upset because he is being confronted by a level of distress he cannot accommodate. He isn't a therapist; he is a teacher in the middle of his school day. And I'm not a therapist either, remember? I don't know what I'm doing. Maybe Heya shouldn't write any poems. Maybe the trauma of seeing your sisters die is something you should raise only in a safe place: a hospital, perhaps. Maybe a poem doesn't count.

I ask Shakila. She says, in her husky, precise, Farsi accent, 'Three sisters? Three is a lot.' And sits looking at her pretty hands for a while. Then she says, 'You know, in Damascus, those are Hazara boys who do the bombing. There is a regiment of them, Miss, there.'

I did know that. In Iran, the authorities round up illegal Hazara labourers and conscript them to fight for Assad in Syria, boys the same age as Shakila, very often. But it had hardly occurred to me that Shakila is Shia and Heya is Sunni; that they are from opposite sides of the deep rift in the Middle East. I'd thought of them, simply, as similar kinds of literary girls. Is that the problem? At Ghazal Club, the two girls sat next to each other, and exchanged words in Arabic and Persian.

'I don't think Heya thinks like that at all,' I say. 'Do you? Honestly?'

'No,' says Shakila, and she sighs. 'Not really. I think poems just make her remember. You know? We'll try again. Miss, try an Arabic poem.'

I remember how long the head poem took to write, and I try again. Shakila is right that we should have a dual text. I go to Mahmoud Darwish, the great Palestinian poet who is also, thankfully, lyrical, accessible, and widely available on the internet in two languages. I pick some sections from 'Under Siege', about the war in Palestine. I manage to stick the Arabic original to the right-hand margin of my A4 sheet. I make several copies. Then, without a word to the form teacher, Shakila and I ambush Heya when we

know she has a study lesson, and entice her to the conference room, which we have booked in advance, and which
is carpeted and quiet. We feed her grapes. We whip out
the Darwish poem. We hope.

It works. In minutes, Shakila and Heya are swapping
words in Arabic, Persian, and English, working out, first,
what has been done in the English translation, what the
soul of the poem means. Then they start. Heya, I notice,
is writing straight into English, with occasional glances at
the dictionary on her phone, rather than, as she has before,
writing in Arabic and translating afterwards. She writes
about her street as it used to be, her house, her courtyard,
the trees that grew there, the birds . . . (But everyone from
Damascus writes about the birds. When I see the images
of the bombed city now, I worry about the doves, where
they have gone.)

Shakila sticks close to the Darwish text, and makes a
sophisticated Persian/English version of its ending – how
do you create a new compound noun for 'Homeland'? Heya,
meanwhile, returns to her own story. We are back in the
house in Damascus, the bomb, the noise, the dust, the
blood. 'How I held my sister's body,' she writes, as the bell
goes, and she hands me the piece of paper. The form teacher
will find out what I did, I know, and we will be back at
square one.

Except this time Heya is not crying.

For the next four weeks Heya does not/cannot/will not come
to Poetry Group, or even to look at the proofs of the
anthology I am putting together, heavily featuring her

poems, and I have nearly given up on her when two little Syrian sisters approach me with a wad of A4 'for the book'. The book – one I'm making with the university for a translation project – is practically on press, and so I can't include their work. I explain this to the little sisters and they shake their heads. They will not have it.

So we call up Google Translate. I call in Shakila and the Professor of Arabic to make versions of the poems. Gosh, they're good. Four poems making a word play on 'Homeland' . . . another lamenting the view from the window . . . an idea occurs to me. When the girls come back to me, two meek black hijabs, two pairs of specs, I show them the Mahmoud Darwish print-out. They nod at once. Yes, Heya showed them that. She helped them write their poems.

And when the book is printed, no one could be prouder than Heya; she can hardly let it out of her hands. She asks her whole family to the launch, and they come and bring tabbouleh. She stands in front of them and reads her poems, in Arabic and in English, the one about dawn, the one about her sisters, and the new one. We clap and clap.

A week later a small Syrian boy appears, looking for me. He is from the same set of government-sponsored refugees as Heya, but has much less English, as if he were refusing to learn it. I know him, though. I think the whole school does. He is very short and exceptionally beautiful, with tawny hair and skin and huge, fringed, smoky blue eyes. At break times he plays basketball with the Year 11 girls, their mascot and pet, and I've seen him break-dance for them, tiny taut body thrown up and backwards, truly wild, reckless, almost feral. He was two years in the jungle in Calais. Firmly, now, he hands me a poem, written in Arabic. 'For the book,' he says, and I try to explain that the book is published already and there won't be another one till next year and— 'Poem,' he says firmly.

So I tell him to go along to the library and borrow Heya. She comes, modest and smiling. She says the writing is good, good Arabic, and gets out her phone, loaded with Google Translate. I put a new document up on the screen.

'They carried her in a black tent to my house,' says Heya, in her high, careful little voice. I stare. Then a news bulletin comes to mind: a funeral in the Middle East, a body wrapped in black.

'Oh,' I say, 'like a shroud? Like a funeral?'

'Yes,' says Heya. 'Funeral. And now we need the word for grave. But not grave. The word for the hole for the grave.'

And so we go on, the small boy – and he is such a very small boy – looking anxiously from one face to another. Working with Heya is nearly as good as working with Shakila. She doesn't have so many words, but she certainly has the same drive for precision. Soon, we have this:

They carry you in a black shroud to my door.
This is your plot, Syria, strung with ropes, ready,
These are your deserts, and your mountains,
And all the people calling your name.

Syria, you must say to the mourners: my name
Is not on the grave. Though Daddy is martyred

And will not come back through the door,
Though from behind the cloth comes the wail of pain.

The name of Syria is not on the grave.

'Is it a good poem?' asks Heya.

'Yes,' I say, 'I think so. But it is . . . surprising. It sounds very old.'

'I will tell him it is a good poem,' says Heya. And she does, in Arabic, and he smiles.

'Tell him,' I say, 'that he has a very grown-up poet living inside him.'

She does, and this makes them both laugh.

Then I say, 'Tell him, please, that if you are a poet it is hard to lose your language, very, very hard. But he can get it back. He can still write poems. He can learn to write in English too.'

'We can find his poem,' says Heya.

And she passes on the messages, and the small boy cries.

Acknowledgements

Dear Colleagues: this book is full of my debts to you. I would name you all, but then the kids would be more identifiable, and I know you always put them first. So if you have worked with me, please imagine your name here and accept my thanks.

I am very grateful to Zoë Waldie and Kris Doyle for their guidance and excellent edits, and to Paul Baggaley and all at Picador for their unstinting support over many years.